Essentials of Contract Drafting and Negotiation for Construction Professionals

Essentials of Contract Drafting and Negotiation for Construction Professionals

Edited by Gary Soo and Peter Cheng

HKU PRESS
香港大學出版社

Hong Kong University Press
The University of Hong Kong
Pok Fu Lam Road
Hong Kong
https://hkupress.hku.hk

ISBN 978-988-8754-11-3 (*Paperback*)
ISBN 978-988-8754-16-8 (*Hardback*)

British Library Cataloguing-in-Publication Data
A catalogue record for this book is available from the British Library.

Digitally printed

To all construction professionals

who see the benefits of legal training in bringing a difference to their work

Hong Kong Legal Training Institute

Contents

Preface

Essentials of Contract Drafting and Negotiation for Construction Professionals is a practical and user-friendly guide designed for construction professionals involved in contract drafting and negotiation. Knowledge of how to draft an effective contract is crucial in order to consolidate and properly document the ideas agreed upon by the contracting parties. This book is an essential tool for creating contracts which are sound in both form and substance, as clarity and precision are no less important than legal correctness in avoiding traps and pitfalls in contract negotiation and enforcement.

This book contains six chapters and is best read with its companion text, *Construction Contract Essentials in Hong Kong*, which together provide readers with a thorough understanding of the legal aspects of the successful drafting and development of a construction contract. Chapter 1, 'Overview and Features of Construction Contracts', highlights the specific points to note in contract drafting and negotiation. Chapter 2, 'The Interpretation of Construction Contracts', illustrates how the legal rules of interpretation apply to construction contracts. Chapter 3, 'Pre-contractual Documents, Communication, and Misrepresentation', demonstrates the essential elements to be included, and elements to be avoided, in a contractual document. Chapter 4, 'Structure and Format of Construction Contracts', explains the different forms of construction contracts. Chapter 5, 'Contract Drafting Techniques and Common Mistakes', and Chapter 6, 'Important Clauses in Construction Contracts', explain the drafting of those vital clauses in a construction contract and their negotiation while providing techniques to attain clarity and avoid common mistakes in drafting.

It is hoped that this book will serve to enhance and refresh the knowledge of legal practitioners, construction professionals, students, and the public at large in the legal aspects of construction-related industries for the advancement of knowledge and the enhancement of their practical skills.

Gary Soo

Contributors

(In alphabetical order)

Peter Cheng is a director of a listed property developer. He has a wealth of experience in property development and management. He took an active part in the development of the Hong Kong Convention and Exhibition Centre, the Macau Ferry Terminal, and the drainage construction project in Macau. He has also made substantial contributions to property projects in mainland China. Peter has experience mediating both commercial and family disputes and is on the lists of the mediators of Hong Kong Mediation Accreditation Association Limited (HKMAAL), Hong Kong International Arbitration Centre (HKIAC), Hong Kong Mediation Centre (HKMC), and Financial Dispute Resolution Centre (FDRC).

Solomon Lam is a practising barrister, chartered civil engineer (CEng), a member of the Institution of Civil Engineers (ICE), a fellow of the Hong Kong Institute of Arbitrators (HKIArb), a member of the Chartered Institute of Arbitrators (CIArb), and a mediator accredited by HKMAAL and HKIAC. He practises mainly in the areas of construction, arbitration, personal injury, building management, and land disputes.

Ronald Pang has been a practising barrister in Hong Kong since 2016 and is developing a broad civil and commercial practice. He has, in different capacities, worked on cases involving land, trusts, wills and probate, shareholder disputes, insolvency, and matrimonial matters. He has also been instructed to provide advice on Hong Kong law in matters involving cross-border litigation disputes.

Gary Soo is an international arbitrator, practising barrister, and chartered engineer. He has practised civil litigation involving commercial and construction disputes and arbitration for 20 years. From 2008 to 2010, he served as the secretary-general of the HKIAC. He was also the president of the HKIArb from 2006 to 2008 and from 2010 to 2011.

Isaac Yung has been a practising barrister in Hong Kong since 2015. He maintains a broad practice across the full spectrum of civil disputes, recently focusing on general commercial disputes, land related disputes, trusts, and probate matters. Between 2020 and 2021, he served as a judicial associate to the Court of Appeal and assisted civil appellate judges by researching points of law and analysing and writing memoranda on appeals and leave applications. He will do so again in 2022.

1
Overview and Features of Construction Contracts

Solomon Lam

1.1 Construction contracts *always* need careful handling. From negotiating to drafting, from administering to applying, and from disputing to settling the terms and meaning of what is stipulated and what is not provided, a construction contract calls for thoughtful consideration and proper understanding. This is partly due to the unique features of construction contracts, as compared to other commercial contracts; it is also due to the fact that the amounts and consequences at stake and the uncertainties involved are often substantial.

Aim and Structure of This Book

1.2 Contracts are important instruments governing commercial activities in Hong Kong. The guiding principles of contracts must be properly understood by those operating them to avoid legal pitfalls. Apart from negotiating and performing contracts, it is also important for contracting parties to beware of the guiding principles in drafting and interpreting contractual documents.

1.3 Construction contracts involve complex activities and huge sums of money. It is therefore particularly important for contracting parties in the construction industry to understand the guiding principles of drafting and interpreting construction contracts. This applies to construction professionals such as architects, engineers, surveyors and project managers, as well as executives, managers and directors of construction entities and those involved in the daily administration or performance of construction contracts. This is also vital for construction lawyers who may find drafting and dealing with construction contracts to be particularly challenging in view of the technical nature and unique features of construction projects.

1.4 With a practical and pragmatic approach, through case review and practical examples, this publication aims to enhance, update, and refresh the essential legal knowledge for legal practitioners, construction professionals and personnel, construction law academics and students, and the public-at-large who may be involved with or affected by the construction industry.

1.5 There are six chapters in this book:

Chapter 1: Overview and Features of Construction Contracts

Chapter 2: The Interpretation of Construction Contracts

Chapter 3: Pre-contractual Documents, Communication, and Misrepresentation

Chapter 4: Structure and Format of Construction Contracts

Chapter 5: Contract Drafting Techniques and Common Mistakes

Chapter 6: Important Clauses in Construction Contracts

1.6 Chapter 1 serves as an introduction to this publication. It discusses the features of construction contracts as compared to other contracts. It provides the legal fundamentals of the interpretation of construction contracts. It also examines new legal issues arising out of the latest trends of adopting Building Information Modelling ('BIM'), Modular Integrated Construction ('MIC') and NEC4 in relation to the Hong Kong construction industry.

1.7 Chapter 2 discusses the legal principles of contract drafting and negotiation. It explains the *contra proferentem* rule, the parol evidence rule and the *ejusdem generis* rule and illustrates their relevance to construction contracts.

1.8 Chapter 3 discusses the legal effects of pre-contractual documents and communications, and their importance in the interpretation of construction contracts. It includes discussion of the various effects of letters of intent, letters of comfort and the concept of good faith in contract negotiation and drafting.

1.9 Chapter 4 discusses the structure and format of construction contracts. It covers the different types of contractual documents commonly used in the construction industry and their legal effects. It also discusses the legal effects of different contract terms typically found in standard form construction contracts. It further deals with the legal issues in relation to missing items, consideration in issuing certificates and concurrent delays, all of which are important topics commonly associated with disputes involving construction contracts adopting such standard forms.

1.10 Chapter 5 discusses different contract drafting techniques relevant to construction contracts and the common mistakes by contracting parties leading to disputes.

1.11 Chapter 6 discusses some particularly important clauses of construction contracts and how arguments over such clauses are resolved in arbitration or in court. It covers delay clauses, variation clauses, liquidated damage clauses, dispute resolution clauses and arbitration clauses.

Construction Contracts Follow General Contract Laws

1.12 The laws governing construction projects are the same laws that apply in other spectrums of substantive matters. The laws governing construction contracts follow the general principles of contract law.

1.13 The areas of general contract law principle pertinent to construction contracts, which are often argued by the parties in arbitration and in court, include:

- interpretation of contract terms
- breach of contract and damages
- missing items
- delays
- liquidated damages
- variations

1.14 It is important for construction professionals and stakeholders to understand the relevant legal principles and their effects before they can properly negotiate and draft their construction contracts. Therefore, with reference to the construction industry context, these general principles are covered in this book.

1.15 Apart from general principles, this book will cover specific issues and pitfalls that should be addressed by parties negotiating and drafting construction contracts.

Features of Construction Contracts

1.16 Construction works are highly technical by nature. Additionally, new techniques and methods of construction are regularly introduced, new approaches to contracting are adopted, and new applications of data and technology feed continuous innovation in all areas. Along with the positive side of these developments comes a new frontier of risks associated with trespassing on new paradigms. For example, the use of Building Integrated Modelling ('BIM') is meant to help eliminate errors (such as buildability of the design) prior to construction but it also brings in new forms of errors (database update error) when put to use. The adoption of new construction technologies is always challenging, technically and legally. The wide adoption of Modular Integrated Construction ('MIC') brings new perspectives and focal areas for potential contractual confrontations.

1.17 Construction projects often last for a long period of time, in terms of years, and many exigencies can arise during the contract period. The uncertainties and changes may come from outside the project, such as due to an economic downturn, a change in society's expectations or even a pandemic. The longer the project duration, the greater such risks.

1.18 Due to the industry practice of division of labour and subcontracting, a construction project involves many contracting parties. There can be multiple layers of subcontracting and their respective rights and obligations may affect each other. There are also third party professionals like architects, engineers and surveyors who are not parties to the construction contract between the contractor and the employer, but the construction contract confers roles, functions and powers upon them, and thus the rights and obligations of the contractor and the employer are affected by these third parties.

1.19 All of these features make construction contracts a specialised area of their own.

1.20 Accordingly, the way construction contracts are put together is also specific to the industry. This is particularly so when standard forms of contracts are adopted. Very often, project-specific and in-house amendments are made to the standard forms of contracts, drawing from previous experience and lessons learnt. Not all of these amendments have been tested in court or in arbitration. How to read them together with the rest of the standard conditions of contract, the standard methods of measurement, the general specifications and the standard drawings are always challenging, particularly when thorough consideration of them may not always be possible due to time constraints in drawing up a tender. The number of pages involved in construction contracts is always stunning and references in it to the various codes, standards and guidelines are quite nonstop.

Types of Procurement Methods

1.21 Apart from the general features of construction contracts, it is also important for lawyers, construction professionals and other involved parties to understand the usual procurement methods and the methods of payment associated with construction contracts, in order to better understand the essentials of contract drafting and negotiation discussed in this publication.

1.22 The more common procurement method is usually referred to as the traditional procurement method. In this method, the employer engages the architect or engineer to translate its wishes into detailed plans and the surveyor to measure the amount of labour and materials necessary to complete the works according to the plans and set them out in the bills of quantities.[1]

1. Stephen Furst and Sir Vivian Ramsey, *Keating on Construction Contracts*, 10th ed. (Sweet & Maxwell, 2016), para. 1-030.

1.23 The works are carried out by the contractor under the supervision of the architect or the engineer. It is usual for interim payments to be made from time to time as certified by the architect or the engineer. These interim payments are subject to retention money which will be released after the defect liability or maintenance period as determined by the architect or the engineer.[2]

1.24 It can be seen that, in the traditional procurement method, the third party contract administrator (usually the architect or the engineer named in the construction contract) is very important in determining the rights and obligations of the contractor and the employer.

1.25 Another common type of procurement method is design and build. It is also referred to as turnkey contract. In design and build contracts, the contractor offers to perform (some of) the duties of the architect, engineer or other professionals. It is argued that this allows time and costs to be saved as compared to the traditional procurement method.[3] Since the contractor is also responsible for the design of the works, design and build contracts usually impliedly or expressly impose an additional obligation onto the contractor to complete the works, which are to be fit for purpose.

1.26 Nowadays, it is more common for parties to adopt a different procurement method such as management and construction management contracts. The main feature of such arrangements is that there is a management contractor or construction manager who generally does little or no direct construction work, instead organising and co-ordinating those who do. The management contractor is usually paid the prime cost of the works plus a fee which may be increased by a bonus related to the amount by which the actual cost of the works is less than a target cost. The works themselves are carried out by works contractors who may be subcontractors of the management contractor or in direct contract with the employer. This type of procurement method is more akin to the traditional procurement method.[4] The drafting and negotiating approaches to this type of procurement are certainly not the same as those under the more traditional method.

1.27 Apart from procurement method, it is also important to understand the payment method of construction contracts. Most construction contracts are paid on lump sum basis or by remeasurement according to bills of quantities. Sometimes, contractors may be paid on cost-reimbursement basis.

2. Stephen Furst and Sir Vivian Ramsey, *Keating on Construction Contracts*, 10th ed. (Sweet & Maxwell, 2016), para. 1-030.
3. Stephen Furst and Sir Vivian Ramsey, *Keating on Construction Contracts*, 10th ed. (Sweet & Maxwell, 2016), para. 1-035.
4. Stephen Furst and Sir Vivian Ramsey, *Keating on Construction Contracts*, 10th ed. (Sweet & Maxwell, 2016), para. 1-044.

1.28 Lump sum contracts mean that the contractor is to be paid a fixed price upon completion of a defined scope of works. The scope of works is defined in drawings and specifications, imposing a responsibility on the contractor to measure the materials correctly and to prepare for the method of construction at the tender stage. A good illustration of the importance in understanding the nature of a lump sum contract can be found in the case of *Hung Wan Construction Co Ltd v Hong Kong Hosing Authority*.[5] In this case, it was held that the scope of works was defined in the drawings and specifications and the contractor should have known the scope in pricing the tender. Therefore, an error in description found in the bills of quantities could not allow the contractor to claim additional payment on top of the contract sum.

1.29 Remeasurement contracts mean the final contract sum is re-calculated at the end of the project by adding up the all the priced items by multiplying the unit rates stated in the bills of quantities with the actual quantities of works. The quantities as stated in the bills of quantities are provisional only; as such, the tender price is for reference only. Therefore, the final payment to be paid by the employer may be much higher than the agreed tender price.

1.30 Cost-reimbursement means the actual cost incurred will be paid by the employer, on top of which the employer pays an additional amount to the contractor as profits or bonus.

New Construction Legal Issues: Building Information Modelling ('BIM')

What is BIM?

1.31 BIM is described by the Construction Industry Council as:

> Building Information Modelling (BIM) is the process of generating and managing building data during its design, construction and during the building or assets life cycle. Typically, the process uses three-dimensional building modelling software to increase productivity of consultants and contractors during the whole asset life cycle. The process produces the Building Information Model database, which encompasses building geometry, spatial relationships, geographic information, quantities and properties of building elements. It is a new way of working using new technology to facilitate project management, better construction process control, cross-disciplinary collaboration, communication with external stakeholders, decision support and risk management.[6]

5. HCCT 21/2010 (unreported, 29 July 2010).
6. https://www.bim.cic.hk/en/bim_in_hk/what_is_bim.

Trend of using BIM

1.32 BIM has been widely adopted in the UK, Europe and North America. In 2012, the government of the UK mandated that BIM be used on all publicly procured projects from April 2016. Similar government mandates have been introduced in Finland, Norway, the US, Singapore and France.[7] Germany will follow in 2020.[8] The use of BIM in mainland China is likewise increasingly adopted in sizeable projects.

1.33 In Hong Kong, paragraph 113 of the Financial Secretary's Budget Speech for 2018–2019 states that the government will adopt BIM technology in the design and construction of major government capital works projects and the Construction Industry Council will formulate BIM technical standards, help equip the industry and encourage the use of such technology in private works projects.[9]

1.34 It was suggested by the Hong Kong Construction Industry Council that the introduction of BIM would make a significant contribution to improving trust in and performance on project delivery.[10]

1.35 The Construction Industry Council published BIM Standards—General, BIM Standards for Architecture and Structural Engineering, BIM Standards for Preparation of Statutory Plan Submissions, BIM Standards for Underground Utilities, and BIM Standards for Mechanical Electrical and Plumbing—in 2019 and 2020, including BIM Dictionary and BIM Exchange Information Requirements (EIR) Template.

1.36 The Construction Industry Council has published a final draft of BIM Standards of Statutory Plan Submission Phase B for comment. Phase A is superstructure plan, foundation plan and demolition plan included hoarding. Phase B is excavation and lateral support plan, site formation plan and ground investigation plan.[11]

Incorporating BIM into the construction contract

1.37 It is noted in Section 1.0—Project Execution Planning of Construction Industry Council's BIM Standards—General that the client BIM requirements may be specified in the scope of services for the lead consultant

7. https://www.geospatialworld.net/article/bim-adoption-around-the-world-how-good-are-we/.
8. Para. 431 of the Interim Report of the Commission of Inquiry into the Construction Works at and near the Hung Hom Station Extension under the Shatin to Central Link Project. See also https://www.pbctoday.co.uk/news/bim-news/bim-level-2/84482/.
9. https://www.budget.gov.hk/2018/eng/budget18.html.
10. Para. 454 of the Interim Report of the Commission of Inquiry into the Construction Works at and near the Hung Hom Station Extension under the Shatin to Central Link Project.
11. https://www.bim.cic.hk/en/resources/publications_detail/69?back=%2fen%2fresources%2fpublications.

and the client requirements shall specify the deliverables for each of the project stages of inception stage, feasibility and planning stage, conceptual design, preliminary design, detailed design, submission to approving authority, construction and as-built. The client requirements may be incorporated into the lead consultancy and main contract tender documentation, to enable the lead consultant and contractor to produce a draft BIM PXP so that their proposed approach, capability and capacity can be evaluated.

1.38 This will be an important consideration in contract drafting in order to incorporate the client's BIM requirements in the contract documents and to make sure that such BIM requirements are consistent with other parts of the contract.

1.39 In the English case of *Trant Engineering Ltd v Mott MacDonald Ltd*,[12] the English Court had the opportunity to look into certain aspects of BIM under an injunction application.

1.40 In a commentary on the *Trant* case published in the Construction Law Journal,[13] it is suggested that an important contractual provision is to clarify who will host the common data environment (CDE). The host of the CDE within a BIM design and construction project plays a vital role since it holds the keys to the data room for the entire project. By denying access to the CDE, the host not only withdraws access to its own designs (which a contract may well permit, for non-payment or for suspension), but potentially also denies access to all other designs held in the CDE, as well as access to the programme, schedules, contracts and so on. The host is therefore the 'gatekeeper' to the entirety of the project information held digitally, meaning that the role is crucial to progress and, therefore, the successful completion of the project.

1.41 It seems that the progress of the whole project may be least affected if the CDE is hosted by the employer, particularly in the case of a dispute like that in *Trant*. However, not all employers have the necessary technical knowledge and capability to fulfil the role of a CDE host.

1.42 It is suggested that the judgment in *Trant* also hints at issues within the scopes of services on BIM enabled projects. While we are yet to receive any clear case law guidance in this area, parties would be wise to scrutinise drafting of both contract terms and scopes of services and question what is actually intended. Being clear, concise and using simple terminology seems a sensible approach while we await further guidance from the court.

12. [2017] EWHC 2061 (TCC); [2017] 7 WLUK 67.
13. (2018) 34 Const LJ 495.

1.43 Another potential area of dispute in relation to BIM is the status of the BIM model—whether it is for reference only or if it has a status equivalent to contract drawings. In construction disputes, there is a common argument by employers that the contractors are required to carry out design development according to the tender drawings such that the design changes could not be variations.

1.44 It was held, in *Multiplex Constructions Pty Ltd v Epworth Hospital*,[14] that once a design component had been 'fully exposed' its design development was at an end. In this case, once 'fully exposed', Epworth could still refine the exposed design at Multiplex's expense. Anything beyond refinement would be a variation except where some other design development had a consequential impact. Therefore, it seems it is a matter of degree relating to the detail level of the BIM model.

1.45 Yet, considering the original intention of BIM, the information contained in the BIM model will be detailed. This may be regarded as a fully exposed design component as held in *Multiplex Constructions Pty Ltd v Epworth Hospital*.[15]

New Construction Legal Issues: Modular Integrated Construction ('MIC')

What is MIC?

1.46 MIC is an innovative construction method. By adopting the approach of factory assembly followed by on-site installation, MIC helps to ease some of the current challenges faced by the local construction industry.[16] Free-standing, integrated modules (complete with finishes, fixtures and fittings) are manufactured and assembled in a factory. By transferring previously on-site construction processes to a controlled factory environment, buildings can be substantially completed off-site. The adverse impacts of weather conditions, scarce labour resources and site constraints can all be substantially reduced. MIC provides a great degree of production quality control, and can improve construction productivity, safety and sustainability.

14. [1996] VCA; BC9603682 (unreported, 28 June 1996).
15. Ibid.
16. http://www.cic.hk/eng/main/mic/whatsmic/aboutmic/; https://www.info.gov.hk/gia/general/201809/24/P2018092400465.htm.

MIC in Hong Kong

1.47 The government announced in September 2018 that its first pilot project adopting MIC had started.[17] This pilot project was the Disciplined Services Quarters for the Fire Services Department at Pak Shing Kok, Tseung Kwan O, which was a project of the Architectural Services Department.

1.48 This pilot project was described as echoing the government's initiative to adopt advanced technology and innovative construction methods to enhance productivity and cost-effectiveness. It aimed to relocate most of the labour-intensive and time-consuming processes to an off-site prefabrication yard with a view to enhancing productivity by minimising the duration of works and demand for construction workers. It also aimed to enhance on-site safety and quality control of projects, as well as reducing adverse impacts on the environment.

1.49 Other government projects include the InnoCell of the Hong Kong Science Park and the Wong Chuk Hang student hostel project of the University of Hong Kong, Multi-welfare Services Complex in Area 29 of Kwu Tung North New Development Area.[18]

1.50 The Housing Authority, in a paper dated 19 February 2019,[19] stated that the Housing Authority would identify a pilot MIC project for public housing. It suggested that using off-site construction has benefits including:

(a) better quality control

(b) site safety enhancement

(c) environmental protection

(d) expediting construction programme

(e) increasing productivity

1.51 For private projects, the Buildings Department published Practice Note ADV-36 in relation to MIC. It provides guidelines on design requirements and quality assurance in delivering MIC projects.[20]

1.52 It is expected that an increasing number of Hong Kong construction projects will adopt MIC.

Disputes involving construction contracts adopting MIC

1.53 Since there is still no standard form of construction contracts specifically designed for MIC, some new legal issues may arise in construction

17. https://www.info.gov.hk/gia/general/201809/24/P2018092400465.htm.
18. https://www.devb.gov.hk/en/home/my_blog/index_id_368.html.
19. Paper No. BC 7/2019, QH 1/2019.
20. Appendix A. https://www.bd.gov.hk/doc/en/resources/codes-and-references/practice-notes-and-circular-letters/pnap/ADV/ADV036.pdf.

projects adopting MIC. What they will be remains to be seen, but experience elsewhere may be drawn upon for insights into drafting and negotiating construction contracts utilising MIC.

1.54 The English case of *Mears Ltd v Costplan Services (South East) Ltd*[21] concerned a dispute in relation to two blocks of student residences that adopted MIC. The original intention was that the rooms for both Block A and B would be of modular construction. In the end, however, all the rooms of Block B were built on site which required some structural modifications. One of the claimant's complaints was that around 50 rooms had been built smaller than was contractually permitted. The factor leading to the reduction in size of the as-constructed modular rooms was different versions of drawings followed by the contractor. The claimant, despite having inspected a prototype module, discovered the defect in size only after the completion of all modules. This case sets out a good example that there changes in construction drawings under MIC construction need proper management.

1.55 Another notable legal issue arising in this case is the plea of estoppel. The defendants raised the point based on the parties' common assumption that the relevant rooms could be built in a contractually conforming way by reference to the sizes shown in the later drawings. The court held that an estoppel by convention as against the claimant could not be established in circumstances where the claimant at the relevant time had not been focusing on particular room sizes, and had not been aware of the deviation from the planning drawings. It was held that mere silence by the claimant was not sufficient. This reinforced that estoppel required some forms of reliance on the representation (such as room sizes in this case) if to be invoked. This case went to the English Court of Appeal not relating to the estoppel issue.[22]

1.56 However, depending on the facts of individual case, estoppel may be established when the contract administrator or his authorised representatives expressly issue instructions inconsistent with the contract drawings. The difference between MIC and traditional contract appears to be that it will be too late to discover any defects relating to the MIC components that are discovered when trying to install the same on site when one adopts MIC. By then, the components have been completed off site ready for transport for installation on site.

1.57 Another English Court of Appeal case, *CIMC MBS Ltd v Bennett (Construction) Ltd*,[23] also involved MIC. In this case, under a contract relating to a proposed new hotel, the main contractor subcontracted to

21. [2018] EWHC 3363 (TCC), [2018] All ER (D) 63 (Dec).
22. [2019] EWCA Civ 502.
23. [2019] EWCA Civ 1515.

the subcontractor the design, supply and installation of 78 prefabricated modular bedroom units. The units were to be made in China and then shipped to Southampton.

1.58 The parties agreed on five milestone payments:

Milestone 1: 20% deposit payable on execution of contract

Milestone 2: 30% on sign-off of prototype room by Park Inn/Key Homes/Bennett in China

Milestone 3: 30% on sign-off of all snagging items by Park Inn/Key Homes/Bennett in China

Milestone 4: 10% on sign-off of units in Southampton

Milestone 5: 10% on completion of installation and any snagging

1.59 The contract contained no specific definition of the term 'sign-off'. There was no payment term in relation to value of works done. The contract came to an end with the liquidation of the developer. The subcontractor sought payment on the basis of the value of the works it had undertaken irrespective of whether the units had reached a stage of completion, at which they could have been signed off, asserting that the terms for interim payments did not comply with section 110 of the Housing Grants, Construction and Regeneration Act 1996, which required adequate mechanism to determine payments. The Court of Appeal reversed the decision of the Queen's Bench and held that the potential involvement of third parties in any sign-off process did not detract from the only applicable criterion, the completion of the prototype or units in accordance with the contract, and the absence of dates of payment did not matter because payments were due on the dates when the milestones were achieved; and that, accordingly, the contract contained an adequate mechanism in accordance with section 110 of the Housing Grants, Construction and Regeneration Act 1996.[24] As a result, the subcontractor's claim on value of work done failed.

1.60 This case illustrates an important consideration in drafting and negotiating MIC related construction contracts, i.e., payment mechanisms. Parties need to be aware that if milestone payments are adopted, the contractor will bear a risk of the employer's liquidation when the modular constructions are underway but have not achieve milestone completion.

1.61 This ties in with the legal arguments in relation to completion and delay of works. It is expected that the completion of construction modules without installation on site cannot be completion of whole of the works. However,

24. Section 110 thereof provides that 'Every construction contract shall (a) provide an adequate mechanism for determining what payments become due under the contract, and when, and provide for a final date for payment in relation to any sum which becomes due. The parties are free to agree how long the period is to be between the date on which a sum becomes due and the final date for payment'.

there are substantial works done after the construction completion of modules even before the transportation to the site. As such, defining milestone completion dates may be an option for the parties to consider.

1.62 In *Mariner International Hotels Ltd & Another v Atlas Ltd & Another*,[25] at para. 27, the Hong Kong Court of Final Appeal held that 'practical completion' meant a state of affairs in which the works had been completed free from any patent defects other than ones to be ignored as trifling.

1.63 In the case of *Hectic Interior Design Ltd v Wong Ching Kai*,[26] the Court held that practical completion was really just another name for the legal concept of substantial completion. In the case of 必瘦站企業管理咨詢(深圳)有限公司 *v Jingo Interiors Design Ltd and Another*,[27] the Court held that completion of the construction contract meant 'practical completion' and applied the definition of practical completion under *Mariner International Hotels Ltd & Another v Atlas Ltd & Another*.

1.64 Other foreseeable disputes can be in relation to the delay in the installation of modules on site due to the employer's fault. This may cause knock-on effects in relation to storage of modules on site and off site and consequential delays to factory production. The parties should consider these possibilities when they negotiate what could be the contractor's entitlement in this regard and when they draft the express terms accordingly.

New Construction Legal Issues: NEC4

1.65 NEC4 was introduced in June 2017. It was stated that the major changes from NEC3 to NEC4 included that NEC4 incorporated a new Design, Build and Operate Contract form, Alliance Contract form, BIM Option and Early Contractor Involvement. The NEC4 Design, Build and Operate Contract aims to combine responsibility for usually disparate functions—design, construction, operation or maintenance—to support operational requirements procured from a single supplier. NEC4 Alliance Contract aims to provide a platform for all parties to work together in achieving client objectives and to share in the risks and benefits of doing so. The BIM Option under NEC4 aims at supporting the use of information modelling. It provides additional clauses to support the management of information model requirements. The NEC4 BIM Option deals with issues of BIM and information ownership, and liability of the parties. Early Contractor Involvement has been launched separately from the contracts in 2015; the ECI is now part of the NEC4 ECC.[28]

25. (2007) 10 HKCFAR 1; [2007] 1 HKLRD 413; [2007] 4 HKLRD 194.
26. DCCJ 5689/2004 (unreported, 30 June 2006); [2006] HKEC 1191.
27. DCCJ 5343/2009 (unreported, 17 May 2012); [2012] HKEC 696.
28. https://www.neccontract.com/About-NEC/NEC4-suite-of-contracts.

1.66 The set of NEC4 standard forms also include a new Professional Services Subcontract, a new Term Service Subcontract, and a new Dispute Resolution Service Contract apart from the new Design, Built and Operate Contract.

1.67 Other changes include changes of terminology, e.g. from 'employer' to 'client', 'works information' to 'scope', 'notifies' to 'informs' etc.

1.68 However, it is observed that NEC4 and NEC3 are largely similar. Particularly, NEC4 clause 10 maintains the provision to 'act in a spirit of mutual trust and co-operation'. The effects of NEC contracts will be discussed in detail in Chapter 4.

1.69 In Hong Kong, the government is encouraging the use of NEC standard forms in public works. The Drainage Services Department (DSD) signed a HK$6.8 million consultancy agreement on 26 June 2018 with Black & Veatch Hong Kong Ltd to undertake investigation of drainage improvement works in Mong Kok. The scope of the consultancy agreement comprises preliminary design for drainage improvement works in Mong Kok and would last for about 18 months. This project adopted NEC4 Professional Services Contract (PSC) Option A for the consultancy, and this is the first NEC4 PSC in Hong Kong. It is said that the new NEC4 PSC enables DSD and the consultant to complete the study of viable schemes for the proposed flood prevention works within the pre-set time frame and advances the implementation of innovative and sustainable flood protection solutions.[29]

29. https://www.dsd.gov.hk/EN/What_s_New/What_s_New/news2773.html.

2
The Interpretation of Construction Contracts

Isaac Yung

Purpose of Interpretation

2.1 At its most basic level, contractual interpretation is the act of ascertaining from the contract the objective intention of its parties at the time the contract was entered into.

2.2 It is important to note the subtle difference between ascertaining the subjective intentions of the parties as opposed to the objective intention expressed in the contract. The courts have emphasised that it is the latter which they are focused on.[1] In doing so, the courts rely heavily on the drafted-up contracts of the parties.

Principles of Contract Interpretation

2.3 The legal principles of contractual interpretation were summarised in *Investors Compensation Scheme Ltd v West Bromwich Building Society*,[2] where Lord Hoffmann set them out as follows:

(1) Interpretation of a contract aims at the ascertainment of the meaning which the contract document would convey to a reasonable person. The reasonable person is one that has all the background knowledge which would reasonably have been available to the parties at the time of the contract.

(2) The background in issue has been famously referred to by Lord Wilberforce as the 'matrix of fact'. This is an understated description of what the background may include. The background includes absolutely anything which would have affected the way in which the language of the contract document would have been understood by a reasonable person, provided that the requirement that it should have been reasonably available to the parties at the time of the contract can be satisfied.

---

1. *Hong Kong & Shanghai Bank Hong Kong (Trustee) Ltd v Chan Lai Wah* [1980] HKCA 268.
2. [1998] 1 WLR 896 at 912H–913F.

(3) There is one exception applicable to the scope of the background in issue. The law excludes from the admissible background the previous negotiations of the parties and their declarations of subjective intent. While the boundaries of this exception are in some respects unclear and remained unexplored, this distinction is made due to the practical policy and, in this respect only, legal interpretation of contract differs from the way one would interpret conversations in daily life. Such background knowledge excluded by the law is admissible only in an action for rectification.

(4) The meaning of words is a matter of dictionaries and grammars; the meaning of the contract document or contract statement is what the parties using those words against the relevant background would reasonably have been understood to mean. Thus, the meaning which a contract document or a contract statement would convey to a reasonable man is not the same thing as the meaning of its words. As such, applying *Mannai Investments Co Ltd v Eagle Star Life Assurance Co Ltd*,[3] the background may enable the reasonable man to choose between the possible meanings of words which are ambiguous, and may even enable to conclude that the parties must, for whatever reason as occasionally happens in ordinary life, have used the wrong words or syntax.

(5) The rule that words should be given their natural and ordinary meaning reflects the common-sense proposition that it is not easily accepted that people have made linguistic mistakes, particularly in formal documents. This is different if one would nevertheless conclude from the background that something must have gone wrong with the language. In such a case, the law does not require judges to attribute to the parties an intention which they plainly could not have had. This is the point made by Lord Diplock in *Antaios Compania Naviera S.A. v Salen Rederierna A.B.*;[4] common sense is to prevail in such a situation.

2.4 It is important to note that the process of interpretation does not stop with the meaning of the words used in the contract.

2.5 Interpretation of a contractual document has come to be known as an iterative process. This is sometimes seen as the sixth principle of contractual interpretation.[5]

2.6 One needs to be mindful of two important points regarding the iterative process. First, the iterative process is not confined to textual analysis but

---

3. [1997] AC 749.
4. In *Antaios Compania Naviera S.A. v Salen Rederierna A.B.* [1985] AC 191, at 201, Lord Diplock stated: 'if detailed semantic and syntactical analysis of words in a commercial contract is going to lead to a conclusion that flouts business common sense, it must be made to yield to business common sense.'
5. Kim Lewison, *The Interpretation of Contracts*, 7th ed. (Sweet & Maxwell, 2020), at [1.01].

also requires placing rival interpretations within their commercial settings and investigating or evaluating their commercial consequences.[6]

2.7 Second, in determining the meaning of words in the contract, one must consider not only the contractual language itself, but also the context of those background facts that are admissible for the purpose of interpreting the contract.[7] This factual context is wider than just the exchanges in the negotiations.

Express Terms

2.8 The first and foremost foray into the construction of a contract is its express terms. These are the terms expressly provided or inserted into the contract. They may be words spoken in oral contracts, or they may be words written out in written contracts; they may even be terms contained in other documents (such as standard forms of contracts) incorporated by reference in oral or written contracts.

2.9 As a primary rule, in the process of interpretation, the express terms will be given their natural and ordinary meaning unless there the contract itself indicates that a special meaning should be ascribed to them.

Implied Terms

2.10 The courts are frequently asked to imply terms into contracts. This may happen when parties to a contract were satisfied with the express terms but left other terms out of the contract, assuming they would nonetheless be part of the agreement.

2.11 In such cases and when disputes arise, or when it turns out that the parties are not on the same page as to their 'common' understanding, or the parties realise that there may be terms in the contract which have not been expressly drafted to address the parties' disagreements, parties may need to invite the court to decide on what in fact they had agreed or meant by the words used in the contract. This may be referred to as implying terms by fact.

Implication of term by law

2.12 Aside from implying terms by fact, terms can also be implied by other means. Indeed, implied terms are often argued on the basis of implication by the facts and by law.

---

6. *Napier Park European Credit Opportunities Fund Ltd v Harbourmaster Pro-Rata Clo 2 BV* [2014] EWCA Civ 984.
7. Kim Lewison, *The Interpretation of Contracts*, 7th ed. (Sweet & Maxwell, 2020), at [1.08].

2.13 The courts may imply a term that has not been stated in recognition of the rights and duties of the parties grounded in reasonableness and necessity.[8] Examples include contractual relationships between a landlord and a tenant or between an employer and an employee. The courts have typically implied a term as a necessary incident of the relationship concerned, unless the parties have expressly excluded it, because the parties may have left a good deal unsaid.[9]

2.14 For example, when a contract with fixed price provides for a contractor to carry out works which are sufficiently described, it will normally be implied that there is a parallel duty to complete the works.[10] In many construction contracts, the contract also contains an express obligation to carry out and complete the works. As to completion, it is not uncommon for the completion to be expressed to be to the satisfaction of the engineer or the architect. In such circumstances, as remarked by Cleary J in the New Zealand Court of Appeal case of *Stratford Borough Council v J.H. Ashman (N.P.) Ltd*,[11] every case depends upon the interpretation of the contract as a whole as to whether, on the one hand, the satisfaction of the engineer or the architect is to be the overriding requirement as to the sufficiency of the work even if it does not conform with the specification, or whether, on the other hand, conformity with the specification and the satisfaction of the engineer of the architect are cumulative requirements. In another New Zealand case, *Major v Greenfield*,[12] McCarthy J said:

> Some of the conflicts to be found in these and in other areas are frankly irreconcilable, and I am satisfied that a way can be found through this jungle only if one keeps steadily in mind the principles of construction of building contracts which were clearly stated in the judgment of this court delivered by Cleary J comparatively recently in *Stratford Borough Council v J.H. Ashman (N.P.) Ltd* [1960] NZLR 503. That judgment emphasizes the necessity to decide primarily whether the contract is one where the satisfaction of the architect is to be the overriding requirement as to the sufficiency and quality of the work done, or whether, on the other hand, conformity with the specifications and the satisfaction of the architect are cumulative requirements. The former interpretation is the one favoured in construing modern

8. *Liverpool City Council v Irwin* [1977] AC 239; *Lee Seng Heng Fish's Gravy & Canning Factory Ltd v Adjective Ltd* [2005] HKCFI 934.
9. *New Castle Investments Ltd v WFC Holding Ltd and others* [2020] HKCA 931 at para. 14, citing Lady Hale JSC (as she then was) in *Geys v Societe Generale, London Branch* [2013] 1 AC 523 at [55] with approval.
10. In *Modern Engineering (Bristol) Ltd v Gilbert-Ash (Northern) Ltd* [1974] AC L 689, 717b Lord Diplock said that a building contract is an entire contract for the sale of goods and work and labour for a lump sum price payable by instalments as the goods are delivered and the work is done. See also the South African case in *Bruens v Smith* [1951] 1 SA 67.
11. [1960] NZLR 503.
12. [1965] NZLR 1035.

building contracts. As a result, even in the absence of express provision that the architect's certificates are to be conclusive, generally those certificates are treated as such. The issue of a formal certificate may not be necessary, 'for a certificate is only a mode of expressing the satisfaction.' Each case, however, depends finally on its own documents, and the difficulties in this present case are in great part a product of the uncertainties presented by the documents.

2.15 In *Samake Construction Co Ltd v Incorporated Owners of Lai Wan Building*,[13] in relation to a renovation contract for a building, the employer had to co-operate and enable the contractor access to a restaurant during reasonable hours to execute the works, or if the employer required the work to be carried out at a time which was unreasonable then it went without saying that the contractor was to perform the work at such time as might be required and be paid overtime.

2.16 In the case of *Tridant Engineering Co Ltd v Mansion Fire Engineering Co Ltd*,[14] there was the usual clause in a subcontract for mechanical and electrical works for a commercial building in Guangzhou that the subcontractor was to proceed regularly and diligently. The court was ready to imply into the contract a term that the subcontractor was to proceed with reasonable diligence as a matter of business efficacy.[15] It was observed that an obligation to complete work by a certain date, in itself, was of little value to the employer if there were serious delays during the construction period indicating that the completion date could not be achieved.

Implication of term by statute

2.17 Terms to an agreement may be implied by statute. For example, a consumer who buys a service by the contract itself is silent on certain aspects may seek to rely on the Supply of Services (Implied Terms) Ordinance (Cap 457) (SSO), which provides that services should be carried out with reasonable care and skill[16] and within a reasonable time if the time of performance has not been fixed,[17] and a reasonable charge should be paid if the charge has not been fixed by the contract.[18]

Implication of term by custom, trade, and usage

2.18 If there is an invariable, certain and general usage or custom of a particular trade or place, the law will imply on the part of one who contracts with

13. [2001] HKCFI 1316.
14. [2000] HKCFI 1.
15. Ibid., at para. 23.
16. Section 5 of the Supply of Services (Implied Terms) Ordinance (Cap 457).
17. Section 6 of the Supply of Services (Implied Terms) Ordinance (Cap 457).
18. Section 7 of the Supply of Services (Implied Terms) Ordinance (Cap 457).

another to contract for him, upon a matter to which such usage or custom has reference, a promise for the benefit of the other party.[19]

2.19 Such implied terms must not contradict the express terms of the agreement and, furthermore, the usage of the implied term must be notorious, certain and reasonable, and not contrary to the law; it must also be something more than a mere trade practice.[20]

2.20 There has been judicial debate as to whether implying terms into a contract is a subject of the construction or interpretation of a contract, or if it is something else.

2.21 It was thought that Lord Steyn had answered this question in favour of the latter possibility when he said: 'The processes of construction and implication of terms are closely linked, but as a matter of legal analysis they need to be kept separate'.[21]

2.22 However, Lord Hoffman said that the implication of a term was 'a matter of construction of the contract as a whole in its commercial context' in *Transfield Shipping Inc v Mercator Shipping Inc*.[22]

His Lordship further elaborated on the implication of terms in *Attorney General of Belize and others v Belize Telecom Ltd and another*:[23]

> [16] [T]he court has no power to improve upon the instrument which it is called upon to construe, whether it be a contract, a statute or articles of association. It cannot introduce terms to make it fairer or more reasonable. It is concerned only to discover what the instrument means. However, that meaning is not necessarily or always what the authors or parties to the document would have intended.
>
> [17] The question of implication arises when the instrument does not expressly provide for what is to happen when some event occurs. The most usual inference in such a case is that nothing is to happen. If the parties had intended something to happen, the instrument would have said so. Otherwise, the express provisions of the instruments are to continue to operate undisturbed. If the event has caused loss to one or other of the parties, the loss lies where it falls.

---

19. Hugh Beale, *Chitty on Contracts*, 33rd ed. (Sweet & Maxwell, 2020), at para. 14-033.
20. Hugh Beale, *Chitty on Contracts*, 33rd ed. (Sweet & Maxwell, 2020), at para. 14-033. See *Kin Shing Engineering HK) Co Ltd v Vinson Engineering Ltd* [2005] HKCFI 260. The defendant had subcontracted works to the plaintiff but refused to pay for the plaintiff's extra work done until it had been verified and its final value certified and argued this was 'common trade, custom and practice'. On the evidence, Reyes J held that such alleged custom was neither 'notorious' nor 'certain'.
21. *National Commercial Bank Jamaica Ltd v Guyana Refrigerators Ltd* (1998) 53 WIR 229.
22. [2009] AC 61.
23. [2009] 1 WLR 1988.

> [18] In some cases, however, the reasonable addressee would understand the instrument to mean something else. He would consider that the only meaning consistent with the other provisions of the instrument, read against the relevant background, is that something is to happen. The event in question is to affect the rights of the parties. The instrument may not have expressly said so, but this is what it must mean. In such a case, it is said that the court implies a term as to what will happen if the event in question occurs. But the implication of the term is not an addition to the instrument. It only spells out what the instrument means.

2.23 Lord Hoffman took the view that 'in every case in which it is said that some provision ought to be implied in an instrument, the question for the court is whether such a provision would spell out in express words what the instrument, read against the relevant background, would reasonably be understood to mean'.[24] This appears to suggest the test for implying terms would be based on a reasonableness test.

2.24 The Hong Kong Court of Appeal appeared to fully endorse Lord Hoffman's view in *Tadjudin Sunny v Bank of America, National Association*.[25]

2.25 However, in *Marks & Spencer plc v BNP Paribas Securities Services*,[26] Lord Neuberger PSC (with whom Lord Clarke, Lord Sumption and Lord Hodge JJSC agreed) appear to caution against reading too much into the observations of Lord Hoffmann in *Belize Telecom*:

> [26] I accept that both (i) construing the words which the parties have used in their contract and (ii) implying terms into the contract involve determining the scope and meaning of the contract. However, Lord Hoffman's analysis in the *Belize Telecom* case could obscure the fact that the construing the words used and implying additional words are different processes governed by different rules . . .
>
> [31] . . . it is apparent that Lord Hoffman's observations in the *Belize Telecom* case . . . are open to more than one interpretation . . . and that some of those interpretations are wrong in law. In those circumstances, the right course for us to take is to say that those observations should henceforth be treated as a characteristically inspired discussion rather than authoritative guidance on the law of implied terms.

2.26 Lord Neuberger PSC restated long held principles in that '[t]here does not have to be 'absolute necessity' for a term to be implied but there should be 'business necessity' (such that the contract would lack commercial or practical coherence without the term) or 'obviousness' (such that, if an

24. Ibid., at para. 21.
25. [2016] HKCA 201.
26. [2016] AC 742.

officious bystander would have suggested the implied term to the parties at the time of contracting, they would have both unquestionably agreed to include it as an express term). This is seen as the test of necessity and terms implied in this manner are also known as terms implied by fact.[27]

2.27 Appearing to prefer the opinion of Lord Neuberger PSC, the Hong Kong Court of Appeal followed the well-established test for the implication of terms in *Lo Yuk Sui v Fubon Bank (Hong Kong) Ltd formerly known as International Bank of Asia Ltd*.[28] It is likely that Hong Kong Courts will continue to follow that established test.

2.28 For construction and other contracts, it is also well-established that terms may be implied.[29] As observed by Lord Bingham in *Phillips Electronique v BSB*,[30] the essence of much learning on implied terms is distilled in the speech of Lord Simon of Glaisdale on behalf of the majority of the Judicial Committee of the Privy Council in *BP Refinery (Westernport) Pty Ltd v The President, Councillors and Ratepayers of the Shire of Hastings*:[31]

(1) it must be reasonable and equitable

(2) it must be necessary to give business efficacy to the contract so that no term will be implied if the contract is effective without it

(3) it must be so obvious that it goes without saying

(4) it must be capable of clear expression

(5) it must not contradict any express term of the contract

2.29 This was applied by the Hong Kong Court of Appeal in *First Shanghai Enterprises Ltd v Dahlia Properties Pte Ltd*[32] and *Yau Chin Kwan & Another v Tin Shui Wai Development Ltd*.[33]

2.30 In the context of construction, and in particular, disruption to progress, there are two special types of general implied terms that are especially relevant. First, there is a duty to co-operate; second, there is a duty not to prevent completion. They are essentially two sides of the same coin.

2.31 Regarding the duty to co-operate, the court will readily imply a term in any contract that the parties shall co-operate to ensure the performance of

---

27. Terms can also be implied by way of custom (see *Hutton v Warren* (1836) 1 M&W 460).
28. In [2019] HKCA 261, the Court of Appeal considered *Trump International Golf Club v Scottish Ministers* [2016] WLR 85 in which the UK Supreme Court lowed the approach of Lord Neuberger in *Marks & Spencer plc v BNP Paribas Securities Services* (supra).
29. *Kensland Realty Ltd v Whale View Investment Ltd and Another* (2001) 4 HKCFAR 381 at para. 23, citing Lord Simon of Glaisdale when delivering the advice of the majority in the Privy Council in *B.P. Refinery (Westernport) Pty Ltd v President, Councillors and Ratepayers of the Shire Hastings* (1978) 52 ALJR 20.
30. [1995] EMLR 472.
31. (1978) 52 ALJR 20 at 26.
32. [2002] 3 HKLRD 461.
33. [2003] 2 HKLRD 1.

their bargain. However, the degree of co-operation required is to be determined with reference to the obligations imposed upon each party by the contract itself.[34]

2.32 In construction contracts, it is quite common for one party to complete certain actions before the other party can perform its obligations under the contract.[35] In these circumstances, there can be implied that a duty to co-operate with each other exists under the contract. It has been said in *Luxor (Eastbourne) Ltd v Cooper*[36] that '[g]enerally speaking, where B is employed by A to do a piece of work which requires A's co-operation, it is implied that the necessary co-operation will be forthcoming'.

2.33 The case of *Yue Po Engineering Co Ltd v Ocean Industrial Co*[37] concerned the supply and installation of commercial kitchen equipment to a restaurant in Nanjing. Applying the principle in *Mackay v Dick & Stevenson*,[38] the court was satisfied in the circumstances of the case that it could be an implied term of the contract that delay caused by the defendant in not placing the site in a fit condition for the plaintiff to be able to perform its role under the contract would excuse any delay by the plaintiff occasioned for that reason.[39] The scope of such an implied term also covers those things that the

---

34. For example, an employer has to appoint an engineer or architect to discharge the functions conferred on him under the contract, as in *Hunt v Bishop* (1853) 8 Ex 675; an employer is to call on the engineer or architect to properly perform the function as a certifier under the contract if he fails to apply the terms of the contract properly, as illustrated in the Australian case of *Perini Corporation v Commonwealth of Australia* (1969) 12 BLR 85 and the New Zealand case of *Canterbury Pipe Lines Ltd v Christchurch Drainage Board* (1979) 16 BLR 76. This may lead to an obligation on the employer to replace a defaulting engineer or architect if such defaults persist, as in *Panamena v Leyland* [1947] AC 428, or to re-nominate a nominated subcontractor that had withdrawn from the works, as in *Percy Bilton Ltd v Greater London Council* [1982] 1 WLR 794. Yet, the employer must not trespass beyond the line as to amounting to interference with the proper performance of the engineer or architect in discharging the duties under the contract, as in *Minister Trust Ltd v Traps Tractors Ltd* [1954] 1 WLR 963.
35. For instance, the contract may require the approval of a certain material by the employer. The contractor cannot go forward without such an approval; the employer, in turn, requires reasonable opportunity for dealing with such an approval.
36. [1941] AC 108. In the Scottish case of *Mackay v Dick & Stevenson* (1881) 6 App Cas 251, Lord Blackburn also remarked that: 'I think I may safely say, as a general rule, that where in a written contract it appears that both parties have agreed that something shall be done, which cannot effectually be done unless both concur in doing it, the construction of the contract is that each agrees to do all that is necessary to be done on his part for the carrying out of that thing, though there may be no express words to that effect.'
37. [001] HKCFI 163.
38. (1881) 6 App Cas 251.
39. As explained by Thomas J in *North Sea Energy Holdings NV v Petroleum Authority of Thailand* [1997] 2 Lloyd's Rep 418, at 430: 'Although the Court will often readily imply a term that the parties should co-operate to ensure performance of their bargain, it is clear that such a term must satisfy the test for implication and that implication is not inevitable. . . . what is made clear in all the cases is that a duty to co-operate will only arise if a term can be implied to that effect. Thus, the issue is whether the implied term . . . satisfies the legal test of strict necessity. In doing so, it is useful to apply the 'officious bystander': or the 'business efficacy'

engineer or architect has to carry out to enable the work to be performed by the contractor. These include the issuing of instructions, drawings, and design details in reasonable time to the contractor. All the circumstances of the case must be considered, in particular, the knowledge of the employer or the notice by the contractor, in order to decide what is reasonable. No doubt in most cases, in which information is requested, the perceived need of a contractor will coincide with actual need, but this may not be the case. In *Royal Brompton Hospital National Health Service Trust v Hammond & Others*,[40] it was remarked that, when implying such a term, what had to be construed was to impose an obligation to provide the drawings when necessary in the sense that the drawings had to be provided when actually necessary, as opposed to when they were perceived to be necessary. The obligation of the contractor to warn the employer of design failures may also be regarded as a manifestation of the duty to co-operate. Yet, it seems that the implied term must not be one that is too loose to be implied. In *Neodox Ltd v Borough of Swinton and Pendlebury*,[41] in relation to an implied term, Diplock J observed that the time for provision of information did not depend solely upon the convenience and financial interests of the contractor, but also upon the point of view of the architect, his staff, and the employer. These observations deal with requests that are either premature or made late and cause inconvenience. In *J & J Fee Ltd v The Express Lift Co. Ltd*,[42] in respect of a domestic subcontract, a term was implied to provide the subcontractor with information concerning the subcontract work in such a manner and at such times as was reasonably necessary for the subcontractor to have it in order to fulfil the obligation under the subcontract.

2.34 In recent years, there has been a growing emphasis on good faith in construction contracts. The use of good faith dispute resolution techniques such as partnering is gathering force in Hong Kong and new forms of standard contracts, such as the New Engineering Contract (NEC) in the UK do include express clauses providing, for example, that all involved 'shall act as stated in this Contract and in a spirit of mutual trust and co-operation'.[43]

2.35 In many common law jurisdictions, such as England and Wales, there is no generally applicable doctrine of good faith such as can be found in the

tests as an aid in this task (see *Society of Lloyd's v Clementson* [1995] LRLR 307, at p. 330). I must also have in mind the consideration that the law can enforce co-operation only in a limited degree and to the extent that is necessary to make the contract workable: see *Mona Oil Equipment and Supply Co Ltd v Rhodesia Railways* Ltd (1949) 83 Ll L Rep 178 at 187).'

40. [2002] EWHC 2037.
41. (1958) 5 BLR 34.
42. (1993) 34 Con LR 147.
43. Clause 10.1 of NEC3 Contract.

case of legal systems like United States or Germany.[44] Whether this may affect the operation of the duty to co-operate is yet to been seen. However, the conduct to be expected from an employer and from a contractor is evolving to suit the changing culture and circumstances of the construction industry.

2.36 As to the duty not to prevent completion, as noted in *Stirling v Maitland*,[45] 'if a party enters into an arrangement which can only take effect by the continuance of a certain existing state of circumstances, there is an implied engagement on his part that he shall do nothing of his own motion to put an end to that state of circumstances under which alone the arrangement can become operative'.[46] Whether these implications are made is still dependent upon the nature of the contract.[47]

2.37 This 'prevention' principle was discussed by the Hong Kong Court of Final Appeal in the case of *Kensland Realty Ltd v Whale View Investment Ltd & Another*, a case concerning the sale and purchase of a property.[48] The vendor was selling as a confirmor, i.e. a vendor confirming the sub-sale to the eventual purchaser. The sale and purchase agreement provided that time was of the essence. In the agreement, there was a clause that vendor could direct how the balance of the purchase price was to be paid, but the

44. Yet, implied terms have been utilised to somehow bypass the harshness of the situation. For instance, in *Timeload v British Telecommunications Plc* [1995] EMLR 459, at the time when the defendant was the sole provider of a directory enquiries service for telephone subscribers, it was implied into the contract with the plaintiff who was allotted the number 0800 192192 which was very similar to the defendant's own directory enquiries number that the defendant should not be able to exercise power under the contract to terminate the contract without demonstrable reason or cause for doing so.
45. (1864) 5 B&S 840. Likewise, in *McCarrick v Liverpool Corporation* [1946] 2 All ER 646, it was said that 'in any contract, whatever its nature, it is a general rule that, if the thing agreed to be done cannot effectually be done unless both parties concur in it, the proper construction of the contract requires the implication of a term that each agrees to do all that is necessary to be done on his part for the carrying out of that thing'.
46. For example, an employer does not impliedly warrant the fitness of the site regarding compliance with health and safety requirements as in *Alridge c. Grand Actual* (1996) 55 Con LR 91; an employer is not normally responsible for the delay by a nominated subcontractor chosen by it as in *Leslie & Co Ltd v The Managers of the Metropolitan Asylums District* (1901) 68 JP 86. Interference with third party may also be sufficient ground to find a breach of the implied duty not to prevent completion as in *Acrow (Automation) Ltd v Rex Chainbelt Inc* [1971] 1 WLR 1676.
47. For illustration, it seems that there can be implied such a term on the employer for not acting to disqualify the engineer or the architect as in *Sutcliffe v Thackrah* [1974] 2 AC 727; that there can be an implied duty on a superior contractor not to prevent or hinder the subcontractor from carrying out subcontract works in accordance with the subcontract as in *Jardine Engineering Corp Ltd v Shimizu Corp* [1992] 2 HKC 271, where Kaplan J gave an example by stating: 'In my judgment, where you have a time clause and a penalty clause, it is always implied in such clauses that the penalties are only to apply if the builder has, as far as the building owner is concerned, and his conduct is concerned, that time accorded to him for the execution of the works which the contract contemplates he should have.'
48. [2002] 1 HKLRD 87.

clause was silent as to when such direction was to be given. Completion of the sale and purchase was due to take place by 1:00 pm but, despite earlier requests, it was not until after 11:00 am that the vendor's solicitors gave a split cheque direction. The cashier orders were not delivered to the vendor's solicitors until 1:06 pm and the vendor refused to accept them as the deadline for completion had passed.

2.38 The court held that, if the agreement was silent as to when the split cheque direction should be given, business efficacy demanded that there be an implied term that the direction must be given so as to allow the purchaser's solicitor reasonable time to comply with it, prior to the time for completion.

2.39 It was also held that in assessing what was a reasonable time, account must be taken of all matters which both parties were, or might objectively be taken to be, aware of at the time of making the contract. In the judgment of Ribeiro PJ, it was remarked that these facts bring into play rules derived from the long-established legal principle that 'a person is not permitted to take advantage of his own wrong'. There are however two limitations on the operation of this principle. First, it is necessary to show that the relevant party's 'wrong' involves its breach of the contract in respect of an obligation owed to the other party.[49] Second, it is necessary to show that the contractual rights or benefits which the party in question is seeking to assert or claim arise as a direct consequence of that party's prior breach.[50]

2.40 These cases indicate that reliance on express terms is more straightforward than reliance on implied terms, which, when disputed by the other side, need to survive the scrutiny of the court before they can be held to have been inferred from the parties' agreement.

49. Thus, in *Luxor (Eastbourne) Ltd v Cooper* [1941] AC 108, where an estate agent was engaged on terms that he would be paid commission if he brought about a sale, the House of Lords refused to imply a term to inhibit the owners from disposing of their property themselves or through other channels, thereby preventing the agent from earning commission. It was stressed that the owners were quite entitled to dispose of their property and, in doing so other than through the agent, breached no obligation owed to the agent. Also, as illustrated in *Computer Staff (APEX)* [1983] 2 AC 180, breach of a duty owed to a third party to the contract, whether contractual or non-contractual, does not in itself suffice.

50. This requirement is illustrated in the Australia case of *Nina's Bar Bistro Pty Ltd v MBE Corp (Sydney) Pty Ltd* [1984] 3 NSWLR 613, a case involving the sale of a restaurant subject to the parties' obtaining consent from the lessor for the restaurant's lease to be assigned to the purchaser and the parties' being under an obligation to use their best endeavours to secure such consent. Such consent was not obtained and the purchaser was held to be in breach of the best endeavour obligation. The question was whether, in such circumstances, the purchaser was entitled to terminate the contract. On the facts, the court was not satisfied that the purchaser's failure to obtain the consent of the lessors was causally related to such breach, the probability being that such consent would in any event not have been given. The purchaser was therefore held entitled to terminate notwithstanding its prior breach.

2.41 In *Trollope & Colls Ltd v North-West Metropolitan Regional Hospital Board*,[51] a building contract based on the JCT 63 form provided for works to be carried out in three phases, each with a separate contract sum and its own set of conditions. Phase III was to be completed by a specified date but its date of commencement was to be fixed by reference to the completion of Phase I. There was express provision for the grant of extension of time for completion for Phase I but not for the grant of extension of time of completion for Phase III if Phase I was delayed. The contractor contended that a term for extending the date for completion of Phase III in these circumstances should be implied. The UK House of Lords held that no such term could be implied since the express terms of the contract were clear and unambiguous.

Further case illustrations

2.42 In *Hanison Construction Co Ltd v Diamond Term Ltd*,[52] the plaintiff was the main contractor engaged by the incorporated owners of Wylie Court for the renovation and improvement works at Wylie Court, Homantin, Kowloon. The plaintiff engaged the defendant as its subcontractor in relation to certain renovation works at Wylie Court. However, the defendant failed to complete its works and, in any event, renovation works that were done were defective and the plaintiff incurred extra costs to rectify both the incomplete and defective works. Recorder Chan SC had no hesitation in holding that there were implied terms that the defendant would have to carry out the work in a workmanlike manner, and should use materials of merchantable quality and suitable for the job.

2.43 In *Liu Chung Fai and Another v Tin Shui Wai Development Ltd and Another*, the plaintiff purchasers had entered into sale and purchase agreements with the 1st defendant as vendor (who was also the developer). The agreements did not proceed to completion and the plaintiff purchasers alleged that the defendants had, *inter alia*, breached the implied terms. However, the court held that the implied terms the plaintiffs contended for failed for necessity and clarity.[53]

51. [1973] 1 WLR 601.
52. [2006] HKCFI 311.
53. [2006] HKCFI 742. The plaintiffs had in fact argued for a number of implied terms. The court opined that the pleadings relating to the implied term were complicated to start with and the further draft amendments were appreciably worse. As illustration, the implied terms pleaded were as follows: '[21] It is an implied term of the Agreement . . . that if the 1st Defendant misrepresented (whether innocently, carelessly, recklessly, or knowingly) to the Plaintiffs on matters concerning the time of completion of construction of the Development, or the progress of construction, or extension of the time of completion of construction beyond 31st December 1997 by the authorized person, reasonably relied on by the Plaintiffs due to the inequality of access to the relevant information, thereby prejudicing the Plaintiffs' timely exercise of their right to rescind under clause 4(4)(a) of the Agreement or to accept

2.44 The court held the term sought to be implied was unnecessary because it had assumed the vendor was in some way likely to misrepresent the state of completion for the development, otherwise it would not be necessary to provide for that.[54]

2.45 In *Aggressive Construction Company Ltd v Wai Kin Construction Ltd*,[55] the plaintiff had subcontracted timber formwork of a project to the defendant. Disputes subsequently arose between the parties as the plaintiff alleged the defendant had consistently failed to provide sufficient workforce to carry out the subcontracted works, suspended parts of the works at different times, and made threats to abandon or discontinue the works unless the price under the subcontract was revised. As such, the plaintiff, through its solicitors, sent a letter to the defendant indicating acceptance of the defendant's repudiatory breach of the subcontract and terminating the same.

2.46 At trial, the plaintiff argued that the defendant had breached a number of express terms as well as implied terms of the subcontract, i.e., the defendant was not to delay or obstruct the subcontracted work or other construction works at the site of the project and must not act so as to threaten to delay or obstruct the subcontracted work or other construction works.

2.47 On the other hand, the defendant also argued the subcontract had the following implied terms: first, that the plaintiff should give reasonable and sufficient opportunity and time to the defendant to rectify its defaults before the plaintiff exercised its right to terminate under clause 23 of the subcontract;[56] and second, the plaintiff should give reasonable and sufficient prior written notice to the defendant before it exercised its right to terminate the subcontract under clause 23.

2.48 The court rejected the defendant's arguments for implied terms, holding that clause 23 made a clear distinction between the events which called for a written notice of termination and those which did not. To imply a term as stipulated by the defendant would contradict the clear language and defeat the purpose of the clause. Furthermore, such implied terms would

---

repudiation of the 1st Defendant under common law for failure by the 1st Defendant to complete construction by 31st December 1997, then the time limit of 28 days counting from 31st December 1997 under clause 4(4)(b) deeming the Plaintiffs to have elected to wait for completion should be extended to 28 days from the time when the Plaintiffs found out, or could reasonably be expected to find out, the true position and disabused themselves of the misrepresentation from the 1st Defendant.'

54. Ibid., at para. 1.
55. [2018] HKCFI 744.
56. Clause 23 of the subcontract set out the events which triggered the plaintiff's right to terminate the subcontract.

be unnecessary and not obvious.[57] On the facts, the court held the defendant did breach the subcontract and ordered the defendant to pay damages.

Uncertainty of Terms or of Contract

2.49 A contract, or a clause in a contract, may be uncertain if it is unintelligible, if it is meaningless, if the court is unable to select between a variety of meanings fairly attributable to it, where the court is unable to discern the concept which the parties had in mind, or where the terms of the contract require further agreement between the parties in order to implement them.[58]

2.50 Uncertainty is potentially serious as it may prevent a contract from arising at all or may invalidate one particular term in an otherwise valid contract.

2.51 In *Brown v Gould*,[59] it was explained by Megarry J that a provision may be void for uncertainty because it is devoid of any meaning (such as unintelligible collocation of ordinary English words or simply gibberish) or where there is a variety of meanings which can fairly be put on the provision, and it is impossible to say which of them was intended.

2.52 However, courts recognise that they are tasked to construe the written instrument according to canons of construction. In other words, the court must do its best to select, among the contending interpretations, the one that best reflects or matches the intention of the parties as expressed in the language the parties adopted.[60]

2.53 Case law is quite clear that the court is most reluctant to hold an agreement to be void for uncertainty where parties have entered into what they believe is a binding agreement; it will only do so as a last resort.[61]

2.54 The same is applicable to a term of an agreement—the court will be slow to find a term in an agreement void or unenforceable for uncertainty.[62] However, even so, clear and concise drafting is still essential to ensure that the true intention of the parties is recorded and reflected in the contract. Thus, terms or words or provisions in a contract that adversely affect its

57. On the evidence, the court held that the plaintiff had issued letters of warning, site memos and verbal reminders to the defendant requiring it to resume work and send sufficient workers to resume the subcontract before the notice of termination was issued. Therefore, even if there was any implied term as contended by the defendant, sufficient notices and opportunities had been given to the defendant before the termination of the subcontract.
58. Kim Lewison, *The Interpretation of Contracts*, 7th ed. (Sweet & Maxwell, 2020), at [8.10].
59. [1972] 1 Ch 53.
60. *Star Shipping AG v China National Foreign Trade Transportation Corp* [1993] 2 Lloyd's Rep 445 at 452.
61. *Brown v Gould* [1972] 1 Ch 53; *Whitecap Leisure Lt v John H Rundle Ltd* [2008] 2 Lloyd's Rep 216.
62. *Brown v Gould* [1972] 1 Ch 53.

clarity or certainty when reading the contract as a whole are definitely to be avoided.

Ordinary Meaning of Words and Technical Meanings

2.55 A written instrument is typically construed in accordance with its express terms (or in the context also of the implied terms as discussed above). The express terms themselves are to be understood in their plain, ordinary and natural sense, unless they have in respect to the subject matter, as by the known usage of a trade or the like, acquired a peculiar meaning; or unless the context makes it evident that they must in the particular instance, and in order to execute the intention of the parties, be understood in some other special and peculiar sense.[63]

2.56 Therefore, if a word has a customary meaning in a particular trade, evidence is needed to demonstrate that the parties have intended to give the word that meaning before the court will construe the agreement in such manner.[64]

2.57 Similarly, the court recognises that the construction industry, like any specialised industry, may use terms that have specific technical meanings. The court will give effect to such technical, trade or customary meanings if the circumstances indicate that the parties so intended.

2.58 It is also common for words to have multiple meanings. In such case, the proper meaning will be determined by reference to the context in which the word is used.[65]

Reasonableness of the Result

2.59 If an interpretation of a contractual term will lead to an unreasonable result that goes contrary to business common sense, the court will unlikely adopt it. In other words, the reasonableness of the result of a particular interpretation is a relevant consideration in deciding between rival interpretations.

2.60 This is because when parties execute formal documents, particularly when lawyers are involved, there must be a presumption that there are no linguistic mistakes in the document, unless one can conclude from the background that something must have gone wrong with the language used; e.g., the ordinary meaning of the words involve an absurdity, or

---

63. *Robertson v French* (1803) 4 East 130 at 135.
64. *Shore v Wilson* (1842) 9 Cl & Fin 355; *Smith v Wilson* (1832) 3 B & Ad 732.
65. *Schuler LAG v Wickman Machine Tool Sales Ltd* [1974] AC 235.

would lead to clearly unreasonable result, or would impose on the party/parties a duty that it/they could not reasonably be expected to assume.[66]

2.61 In *Wickman Machine Tools Sales Ltd L. Schuler AG*,[67] Lord Reid said:

> The fact that a particular construction leads to a very unreasonable result must be a relevant consideration. The more unreasonable the result, the more unlikely it is that the parties can have intended it, and if they do intend it the more necessary it is that they shall make their intention abundantly clear.

That being said, the United Kingdom Supreme Court[68] has rightly stated that:

> [C]ommercial common sense is not to be invoked retrospectively. The mere fact that a contractual arrangement, if interpreted according to its natural language, has worked out badly, or even disastrously, for one of the parties is not a reason for departing from the natural language. Commercial common sense is only relevant to the extent of how matters would or could have been perceived by parties, or by reasonable people in the position of the parties, as at the date that the contract was made. Judicial observations such as those of Lord Reid in *Wickman Machine Tools Sales Ltd* . . . have to be read and applied bearing that important point in mind.

2.62 In other words, the court is not prepared to 're-write' the contract if a term is unambiguous even if the term itself may be unreasonable.

2.63 In *Newell Curtain Wall & Engineering Co Ltd v Sunyards Engineering*,[69] the plaintiff was the nominated subcontractor of a construction project at Po Lin Monastery at Ngong Ping, Lantau and the defendant was a supplier and fabricator of glass reinforced plastic works (GRP) products.

2.64 By a letter of acceptance, the plaintiff had accepted the defendant's quotation for GRP works. However, such acceptance was conditional upon the defendant obtaining approval from the Po Lin Monastery and their architectural specialist to a mock-up which the defendant would construct in accordance with the requirements and specifications referred to in the plaintiff's letter of acceptance.

2.65 It was the plaintiff's primary case that the requirement for this approval was a condition precedent to the coming into effect of any contract between the parties, and ultimately no approval was obtained for the mock-up.

---

66. *First Shanghai Enterprises Ltd v Dahlia Properties PTE Ltd* [2002] 3 HKLRD 461 at para. 24.
67. [1974] AC 235.
68. *Arnold v Britton* [2015] AC 1619 at para. 19.
69. [2012] HKCFI 1942.

2.66 The plaintiff relied on the following clause: 'The contract will effective upon mock-up approval by the Architect and Po Lin Monastery'.[70] It was argued that the terms in the clause were unambiguous.

2.67 The defendant invited the court to modify the clause, referring to *Permtek Ltd v China Resources Machinery & Equipment. Ltd*[71] However, the court refused to do so because it found the clause to be unambiguous, and acceding to the defendant's request would be contrary to established authorities.

2.68 In the end, the court ruled in favour of the plaintiff and held that the contract was a conditional contract in respect of which the defendant had failed to comply with the condition precedent.

Contra Proferentem Rule

2.69 The *contra proferentem* (Latin: 'against the offeror') rule, in its simplest form, amounts to the resolution of an ambiguity in an agreement that cannot be resolved by other principles of construction. It resolves such ambiguity against interests of the party responsible for putting forward the relevant clause or benefiting from its inclusion in the agreement.

2.70 This rule is to be used as a last resort. If there is no ambiguity or obscurity, there is simply no room for the rule to apply, even if the clause in dispute is neither elegant nor ideal.[72]

2.71 The basis and rationale of the principle is that a person who puts forward the wording of a proposed agreement may be assumed to have looked after his own interests, so that if the words leave room for doubt about whether he is intended to have a particular benefit, there is reason to suppose he is not.[73]

Standard Form Contract Terms

2.72 It has been observed that the use of standard forms of contracts in the Hong Kong construction industry is increasingly prevalent; in fact, some public authorities devise their own standard forms. In particular, standard forms of construction contracts used by employers often embody the relevant views and suggestions and are drafted in consultation of representative bodies of contractors. In such circumstances, it has been suggested that the *contra proferentem* rule should have no application, although perhaps,

---

70. The court did not consider the omission of the word 'become' in any manner to affect the legal purport of the clause as it in no way detracted from what was obviously meant.
71. (1989) 2 HLKR 349.
72. *Bewise Motors Ltd v Hoi Kong Container Services Ltd* (1998) 1 HKCFAR 256 at para. 61.
73. *Tam Wing Chuen v Bank of Credit and Commerce Hong Kong* [1996] 2 BCLC 69.

due to modifications of such standard forms, it may be difficult to completely do without the rule.[74]

2.73 Courts in Hong Kong have not come to a definitive view on this matter, though the above contention finds some support in English law.[75]

Parol Evidence Rule

2.74 The parol evidence rule states that where a contract is made wholly in writing, evidence is not admissible to add to, vary or contradict the written terms.

2.75 It is widely accepted that the parol evidence rule includes all forms of evidence outside the contract itself and is not restricted to merely oral evidence. Thus, any written material such as records of negotiation, draft contracts, etc., would be considered inadmissible under this rule.

2.76 The justification for this rule was identified early on in *Shore v Wilson*:[76]

> If it were otherwise, no lawyer would be safe in advising upon the construction of a written instrument, nor any party in taking under it; for the ablest advice might be controlled, and the clearest title undermined, if, at some future period, parol evidence of the particular meaning which the party affixed to his words, or of his secret intention in making the instrument, or of the objects he meant to take benefit under it, might be set up to contradict or vary the plain language of the instrument itself.

2.77 The rule has generally stood the test of time, as Lord Hobhouse of Woodborough said in *Shogun Finance Ltd v Hudson*:[77]

> The rule that other evidence may not be adduced to contradict the provisions of a contract contained in a written document is fundamental to the mercantile law of this country; the bargain is the document; the certainty of the contract depends on it. . . . This rule is one of the great strengths of English commercial law and is one of the main reasons for the international success of English law in preference to laxer systems which do not provide the same certainty.

74. Gary Soo, *Construction Law and Practice in Hong Kong*, 4th ed. (Sweet & Maxwell, 2018), at para. 6.048.

75. *Tersons Ltd v Stevenage Development Corporation* [1963] 2 Lloyd's Rep 333 at 368. In the context of a contra proferentem argument, Pearson LJ opined that the maxim had little if any application to the case before the court, since the general conditions were not a partisan document or 'an imposed standard contract', but were in a general form in common use prepared and revised jointly by various representative bodies.

76. (1842) 9 Cl & F 355.

77. [2004] 1 AC 919.

2.78 In *Lam Tun Ming v Hu Chun Leung*,[78] MacDougall JA cited with approval the application of the rule as stated in *Chitty on Contracts* (26th ed.):

> [T]he scope of the parol evidence rule is much narrower than at first sight appears. It has no application until it is first determined that the terms of the parties' agreement are wholly contained in the written document. The rule only applies where the parties to an agreement reduce it to writing, and agree or intend that the writing shall be their agreement. Whether the parties did so agree or intend is a matter to be decided by the court upon consideration of all the evidence relevant to this issue. It is therefore always open to a party to adduce extrinsic evidence to prove that the document is not a complete record of the contract. If, on that evidence, the court finds that terms additional to those in the document were agreed and intended by the parties to form part of the contract, then the court will have found that the contract consists partly of the terms contained in the document and partly of the terms agreed outside of it. The parol evidence rule will not apply. If, on the other hand, the court finds that the document is a complete record of the contract, then it will reject the evidence of additional terms. But it will do so, not because it is required to ignore the additional terms or the evidence said to prove them, but because such evidence is inconsistent with its finding that the document does contain the entire terms of the parties' agreement. No doubt, in practice, where a document is produced which appears to be a complete contract, a party will experience considerable difficulty in proving, on the balance of probabilities, that further contractual terms were agreed outside the written terms of the document. But extrinsic evidence of such terms is not ipso facto excluded.

2.79 One can see from the above that the application of the parol evidence rule is more narrow than at first glance. Further limiting the application of the rule are a number of exceptions, some of which are discussed below.

2.80 First, extrinsic evidence is admissible to establish the true meaning of an ambiguous term.[79]

2.81 Second, extrinsic evidence will be admitted to prove a collateral contract to the main agreement in question. This does not offend the parol evidence rule because the collateral agreement neither alters nor adds to the written one, but is an independent agreement.[80] One way to prevent a party from arguing the existence of a collateral contract may be the use of a carefully worded 'entire agreement' clause in the main agreement. A typical boilerplate entire agreement clause may be drafted as follows:

---

78. [1991] 2 HKC 285. The updated reference to *Chitty on Contracts* in the judgment would be para. 13-111 of Hugh Beale, *Chitty on Contracts*, 33rd ed. (Sweet & Maxwell, 2020).
79. *L Schuler AG v Wickman Machine Tool Sales Ltd* [1974] AC 235; *Cheng Kwei Sheng v Li Shek Tong* [1976] HKCA 216.
80. See Hugh Beale, *Chitty on Contracts*, 33rd ed. (Sweet & Maxwell, 2020), at para. 13-116. See also *Bank of China (Hong Kong) Ltd v Fung Chin Kan & Another* (2002) 5 HKCFAR 515.

> This agreement contains the entire and only agreement between the parties and supersedes all previous agreements between the parties respecting the subject matter hereof; each party acknowledges that in entering into this agreement it has not relied on any representation or undertaking, whether oral or in writing, save such as are expressly incorporated herein.

2.82 As evident from the clause, the purpose of an entire agreement clause is to prevent parties from placing reliance on statements other than those set out in the written agreement.

2.83 Third, without an 'entire agreement' clause, it may be open for a party to introduce evidence to show that the written agreement was not intended to be the entire contract between the parties. The burden is on the party alleging that the written document does not represent the full contract to rebut a presumption that it does.[81]

2.84 Fourth, extrinsic evidence will most certainly be admissible to defeat an agreement on the ground of fraud, illegality, misrepresentation, mistake or duress.[82]

2.85 Fifth, extrinsic evidence is admissible to show a condition that had to occur before contract performance. In *Pym v Campbell*,[83] parties signed a written agreement wherein Campbell agreed to purchase an invention from Pym. However, Campbell refused to pay when one of Campbell's engineers did not approve the invention. Pym sued for the purchase price.

2.86 The court held that the parol evidence rule was not applicable in this case because it did not concern the construction of the terms of a contract, but rather whether there was any agreement at all. Hence, evidence of oral negotiations between the parties showing that, prior to signing the agreement, there was mutual understanding that the purchase was only to be made when one of Campbell's engineers had approved the invention was therefore admissible.

2.87 Sixth, extrinsic evidence is admissible to show implied terms of custom or trade usage or past dealings as part of a contract not appearing in the written agreement. In *Hutton v Warren*,[84] a farm tenant claimed that it was the custom of the country that the landlord would give a reasonable allowance for seeds and labour bestowed on the land in the last year of the tenancy. The custom also required the tenant to leave any manure for the landlord. The landlord refused to follow such a custom. The court held in favour of the farm tenant and opined that, 'it has long been settled, that, in commercial transactions, extrinsic evidence of custom and usage is

81. *Gillespie v Cheney Eggar & Co* [1896] 2 QB 59.
82. Hugh Beale, *Chitty on Contracts*, 33rd ed. (Sweet & Maxwell, 2020), at para. 13-125.
83. (1856) 6 E & B 370.
84. (1836) 1 M&W 460.

admissible to annex incidents to written contracts, in matters with respect to which they are silent'.

The *Ejusdem Generis* Rule

2.88 The *Ejusdem Generis* (Latin: 'the same kind') rule stipulates that when general words following particular and specific words, then the general words must be confined to the same category of items (or same class) as referred to in the specific words.

2.89 The principle should be applied in a somewhat restrictive manner as it depends on the assumed intention of the parties to the contract. This is because the general words were likely used to resolve any accidental omissions in the particular category mentioned and were likely not intended to extend to objects of a completely different kind. The adoption of this view is consistent with the approach that the courts consider the contract as a whole.

2.90 In *Century Star (Asia) Ltd v Fortune Goldman Ltd*,[85] clause 2(h) of a tenancy agreement stipulated that the defendant landlord's consent was needed to make any alterations or additions to 'the electrical wirings, fire service, plumbing, drainage, gas and air-conditioning etc. installations or other Landlord's fixtures' during the tenancy period. It was common ground that the plaintiff tenant had removed a cockloft, which had been built without the authorisation of the Buildings Department, in the leased premises without the prior consent of the defendant. Relying on the *ejusdem generis* rule, the court found that the plaintiff tenant had not breached clause 2(h) because the listed items were all legal objects and therefore, all 'other Landlord's fixtures and other fittings' should be restricted to legal objects.[86]

2.91 Another example can be found in *Kone Elevator (HK) Ltd v Citybase Property Management Ltd*.[87] The plaintiff was a manufacturer of lifts and escalators and provided maintenance service to lifts and escalators. The court held that the 'key switch' and 'emergency stop button' were not included within the scope of the plaintiff's maintenance works as stipulated in the clause—'Controller, all Relays, Contacts, Coils . . . and all other control equipment' because the specific words were internal parts of an escalator which came into operation after it had been switched on. Furthermore, none of the specific parts were operated by manual effort. Hence, the general words must only refer to equipment of internal control.

---

85. [2015] HKDC 409.
86. [2015] HKDC 409 at paras. 76–80.
87. [2012] HKCFI 1022 at paras. 100–101.

2.92 The principle is also only applicable when the class to which the general words refer can be restricted. If the court is unable to determine a category based on the general words, then the principle is of no assistance. This can render when and how the principle is to be applied sometimes not immediately clear.

2.93 While clarity in drafting the specific clause is always preferred, so long as it is reasonably clear what the class includes and what it excludes then the principle can be applied. Thus, when a ship captain was unable to deliver goods because the port was rendered inaccessible because of ice, the captain's company attempt to rely on the clause 'any other cause' was rejected because it was determined the class referred to therein included only war and disturbance, and could not apply to ice.[88]

2.94 The principle is to be used in conjunction with interpreting the contract as a whole. In *Transocean Drilling UK Ltd v Providence Resources*,[89] Providence entered into a contract with Transocean, the owner of a drilling rig, to drill an appraisal well. Six months after commencement, drilling operations were suspended because the rig had not been in good working condition on delivery. There was no dispute that this was due to the fault of Transocean. Inevitably, Providence incurred additional spread costs (costs of personnel, equipment and services contracted from third parties). The question was whether Providence's wasted spread costs arising from Transocean's breach of contract were 'consequential losses' and therefore excluded by clause 20 of the contract.

2.95 The critical words were 'loss of use (including, without limitation, loss of use or the cost of use of property, equipment materials and services including without limitation, those provided by contractors or subcontractors of every tier or by third parties), loss of business and business interruption'. The High Court held that the category of the general words was loss of expected profit or benefit to be derived from the use of property or equipment, income or benefit and hence 'spread costs' were not included.

2.96 The High Court decision was overturned by the Court of Appeal.[90] The appellate court questioned the application of the *ejusdem generis* rule because it found that the critical words were 'plainly apt on the face of them to cover' spread costs. In particular, the use of 'without limitation', which was used twice in the same clause, evinced that both parties intended the clause to be wide in scope.

88. *SS. Knutsford, Ltd v Tillmanns & Co* [1908] AC 406. The House of Lords had also held that another clause in the contract had addressed 'ice' and hence, reading the contract as a whole, 'any other cause' would not include 'ice'.
89. [2014] EWHC 4260 (Comm).
90. *Transocean Drilling U.K. Ltd v Providence Resources PLC* [2016] EWCA Civ 372 at para. 17.

Good faith

2.97 The concept of good faith in commercial contracts, including construction contracts, gives rise to interesting questions relevant to the negotiation and drafting of agreements which are generally motivated by profit rather than altruistic imperatives.

2.98 Any person involved with any pre-contractual documents and/or communication with other parties will inevitably have pondered 'good faith'. What does the term mean and how much should each party proffer it? What is the scope of 'good faith'?

2.99 Significant developments in 'good faith' doctrine relevant to commercial contracts, including construction contracts, are as follows.

Background

2.100 As early as the case of *Carter v Boehm*,[91] Lord Mansfield referred to good faith as prohibiting 'concealing what [one] privately knows [in order] to draw the other into a bargain from his ignorance of that fact', holding that this was a 'governing principle . . . applicable to all contracts and dealings'.

2.101 However, this idea gained limited traction as evidenced by subsequent English authorities. For example, Bingham LJ, in *Interfoto Picture Library v Stiletto Visual Programmes*,[92] opined that 'English law has, characteristically, committed itself to no such overriding principle but has developed piecemeal solutions in response to demonstrated problems of unfairness'.

2.102 Similarly, Lord Ackner, in *Walford v Miles*,[93] opined in emphatic terms that good faith, at least within the context of contract negotiation, was 'repugnant to the adversarial position of the parties' and 'unworkable in practice'.

2.103 That is not to say that courts did not recognise or were not mindful of 'good faith' as a principle.

2.104 Subsequent to *Interfoto Picture Library*, Lord Bingham in *Director General of Fair Trading v First National Bank*[94] observed that '[g]ood faith . . . is not an artificial or technical concept; nor, since Lord Mansfield was its champion, is it a concept wholly unfamiliar to British lawyers'.[95]

2.105 An early Hong Kong case which made reference to good faith was *Hyundai Engineering and Construction Co Ltd v Vigour Ltd*.[96] Reyes J considered that

91. (1766) 3 Burr 1905.
92. [1987] EWCA Civ 6.
93. [1992] 2 AC 128.
94. [2001] UKHL 52.
95. *Director General of Fair Trading v First National Bank* [2001] UKHL 52 at para. 17.
96. [2004] 3 HKLRD 1 at para. 99.

parties to a contract were under an obligation of good faith to attempt to resolve a dispute through the agreed contractual process.

2.106 Despite the frequent reference to 'good faith', there has not been a widely accepted common law definition of good faith. Furthermore, it appears to be applicable in only limited circumstances. As a result, it has been the norm for lawyers to advise their clients that any claim based on breach of good faith terms (express or implied) would be very unlikely to succeed.

Good Faith in Negotiations

2.107 Negotiating in good faith simply means making a genuine attempt to reach a deal, rather than simply going through the motions and negotiating for the sake of negotiating.

2.108 The seminal English authority on negotiating in good faith is *Walford v Miles*.[97]

2.109 It was alleged that, pursuant to a lockout agreement, the defendants had agreed not to deal with any third parties in relation to the sale of their business as long as they were negotiating with the plaintiffs. The plaintiffs attempted to justify a claim of lost profits on the transaction by seeking to persuade the court to read into the agreement a positive obligation upon the defendants to negotiate the terms of the sale agreement in good faith. The court found that there was no binding lockout agreement on the facts and that even if there had been, there were no grounds to imply an obligation to negotiate in good faith. Lord Ackner, who gave the leading judgment, opined that, as a matter of principle, an agreement to negotiate in good faith was not generally enforceable under English law because it was 'unworkable in practice as it is inherently inconsistent with the position of a negotiating party. It is here that uncertainty lies.' In gist, a negotiating party is negotiating for the benefits of its rights and interests, rather than of the other party.

2.110 In *Petromec v Petroleo*,[98] Petromec had agreed to upgrade an offshore oil platform in accordance with specifications that were different to those originally agreed between the parties. A clause in the contract provided that Petromec and Petroleo agreed to negotiate in good faith as to the amount of any additional costs.

2.111 Longmore LJ addressed and disposed of the typical objections to enforceability. First, there was little uncertainty as to the outcome of the negotiations because it was possible to clearly establish what the additional costs would be. Second, while it may be difficult in some circumstances to determine what amounted to bad faith withdrawal from negotiations, that

97. [1992] 2 AC 128.
98. [2006] 1 Lloyd's Rep 121.

in itself should not be a good reason for the court not to do so. Third, on the facts of the case, it was clear what the relevant loss would have been.

2.112 A similar preference for the court to enforce an express obligation to use good faith is found in *Cable & Wireless plc v IBM United Kingdom Ltd.*[99] The agreement between the parties included a clause which required them to 'attempt in good faith' to resolve disputes arising between them 'through an alternative dispute resolution procedure as recommended to the parties by the Centre for Dispute Resolution'.

2.113 The court did not accept the argument that the clause was unenforceable due to uncertainty. On the contrary, it was enforceable because it laid out the means by which the good faith attempt should be made. Simply put, if a party refused to participate in the prescribed procedure, it would be in breach of its obligation.

2.114 At first glance, it is easy to conclude after *Petromec* and *Cable & Wireless* that obligations to negotiate in good faith could be regarded as somehow enforceable under English law. However, a closer analysis may reveal that these cases actually disturb very little, if any, established principle.

2.115 In both cases, the parameters and objectives of negotiating in good faith were sufficiently clear that the court could determine whether such obligations could be met. Clearly then, if the parameters and objectives were insufficiently prescribed, then enforceability would be an issue.

Good Faith in Performance of Contract

2.116 English courts appear to give effect to good faith provisions in contracts as long as they relate to actual performance of some contractual obligations.

2.117 Hence, in *Berkeley Community Villages Ltd v Pullen*,[100] a clause that stated '[i]n all matters relating to this agreement the practices will act with the utmost good faith towards one another and will act reasonably and prudently at all times' was interpreted as an obligation to observe reasonable commercial standards of fair dealing in accordance with their actions which related to the Agreement and also as requiring faithfulness to the agreed common purpose and consistency with the party's justified expectations.

2.118 Similarly, in *CPC Group Ltd v Qatari Diar Real Estate Investment Co*,[101] a clause stated that parties 'shall both act in the utmost good faith towards each other in relation to the matters set out in this Deed' and 'use all reasonable but commercial prudent endeavours to enable the achievement of

99. [2002] EWHC 2059.
100. [2007] EWHC 1330 (Ch).
101. [2010] EWHC 15335 (Ch).

the various threshold events and Payment Dates'. The court interpreted these clauses as obligations to adhere to the spirit of the contract, to observe reasonable commercial standards of fair dealing, to be faithful to the agreed common purpose, and to act consistently with the parties justified expectations.

2.119 However, an express clause of good faith does not apply when one party, acting reasonably, exercises a termination at will clause—a good faith obligation is only restricted to those expressly listed actions. Co-operation is required for the performance of a contract, but not for its termination, and hence the good faith obligation does not cut across an unqualified and unconditional express right to terminate.[102]

2.120 Parties wishing certain provisions to be governed by a duty of good faith or reasonableness should expressly state it in the agreement. The English courts have demonstrated that good faith provisions will be construed in a restrictive manner and will certainly offer no assistance to parties wishing to renege from undesirable contract clauses.

2.121 The English courts have made it clear that parties wishing to rely on good faith clauses should make it clear they are doing so. Hence a contract requiring parties to have regard to the partnering principles in carrying out their obligations under the contract, that all dealings be 'open, honest, clear and reliable', and that parties 'work together to achieve a relationship of mutual respect and trust' fell short of meaning parties should act in good faith. Instead, such clauses were merely 'aspirational and motivational' and the avoidance of the term 'good faith' evinced the parties' deliberate choice not to subject themselves to a duty of good faith, a choice which should be respected.[103]

Implication of a Duty of Good Faith

2.122 In *Yam Seng Pte Ltd v International Trade Corporation*,[104] the parties entered into a distribution agreement in which the defendant granted the plaintiff the exclusive right to distribute certain fragrances in specific territories.

2.123 The relationship eventually soured and ended acrimoniously. The plaintiff informed the defendant that it was terminating the contract as the defendant was in breach of the agreement. The plaintiff further alleged that the defendant had breached the agreement because of late shipment of orders, failing or refusing to supply all the specified products, undercutting prices agreed with the plaintiff, and providing false information. The plaintiff argued that there was an implied term of the agreement that the parties

102. *TSG Building Services plc v South Anglia Housing Ltd* [2013] EWHC 1151 (TCC).
103. *Fujitsu Services Ltd v IBM United Kingdom Ltd* [2014] EWHC 752 (TCC).
104. 2013 EWHC 111 (QB).

would deal with each other in good faith. Therefore, the court needed to determine whether a duty of good faith could be implied into the contract.

2.124 Leggatt J[105] took note of the 'traditional English hostility' towards a doctrine of good faith. However, he acknowledged that English law would 'appear to be swimming against the tide' if it refused to recognise a general obligation of good faith, as such a concept was recognised by most civil law systems as well as other common law jurisdictions.

2.125 His Lordship stated that '[a]s a matter of construction it is hard to envisage any contract which would not reasonably be understood as requiring honesty in its performance' and noted that such requirements meet the traditional tests for implying terms.

2.126 His Lordship further opined that the implied term included an obligation to comply with 'other standards of commercial dealing which are so generally accepted that the contracting parties could reasonably be understood to take them as read without explicitly stating them in their contractual document' and that a key aspect of good faith is the observance of such standards.

2.127 Furthermore, the judge explained that another aspect of good faith that can be readily implied into a commercial contract is 'what may be described as fidelity to the parties' bargain'. The judge observed that no contract can ever expressly provide for every event that may happen. Hence, in such circumstances, the contractual language must be given reasonable construction which promotes the values and purposes expressed or implicit in the contract.

2.128 *Yam Seng* is a controversial decision which has generated significant academic debate. A number of English cases have approved and applied *Yam Seng*.[106] However, some judges have expressed reservations about the decision.[107]

---

105. Lord Justice Leggatt was eventually appointed a Lord Justice of Appeal in February 2018 and a Justice of the Supreme Court in 21 April 2020.

106. See for example *Emirates Trading Agency LLC v Prime Mineral Exports Private Ltd* [2014] EWHC 2104 (Comm) and *Bristol Groundschool Ltd v Intelligent Capture and others* [2014] EWHC 2145 (Ch).

107. See for example *Hamsard 3147 Ltd and Anor v Boots UK Ltd* [13] EWHC 3251 (Pat). Interestingly, in *Mid Essex Hospital Services NHS Trust v Compass Group UK and Ireland Ltd (t/a Medirest)* [2013] EWCA Civ 200, the UK Court of Appeal essentially avoided setting out a clear position on *Yam Seng*, though it did not completely close the door on the concept of implied general contractual duty of good faith. Subsequently, in *MSC Mediterranean Shipping Company SA v Cottonex Anstalt* [2015] EWHC 283 (Comm), Leggatt J, though not expressly referring to his decision in *Yam Seng*, noted in passing that 'there was increasing recognition in the common law world of the need for good faith in contractual dealings'. However, on appeal in [2016] EWCA Civ 789, the appellate court stated in thinly veiled critical terms that the court 'had recently reiterated that English law does not recognize any general duty of good faith in matters of contract' and bemoaned any attempts by judges to look for 'some 'general organizing principle' drawn from cases of disparate kinds'.

2.129 An implied duty of good faith will likely be recognised in the performance of a contract where the contract is relational. Such contracts may require a high degree of communication, cooperation and predictable performance based on mutual trust and confidence and involve expectations of loyalty which are not legislated for in the express terms of the contract but are implicit in the parties' understanding and necessary to give business efficacy to the arrangements.

2.130 Relational contracts typically involve parties collaborating on a long-term basis. In *Bates v Post Office Ltd (No 3)*,[108] Fraser J set out the characteristics he thought to be relevant when considering whether a contract was a relational one:

(1) there must be no specific express terms in the contract that prevents a duty of good faith being implied into the contract;

(2) the contract will be a long-term one, with the mutual intention of the parties being that there will be a long-term relationship;

(3) the parties must intend that their respective roles be performed with integrity, and with fidelity to their bargain;

(4) the parties will be committed to collaborating with one another in the performance of the contract;

(5) the spirits and objectives of their venture may not be capable of being expressed exhaustively in a written contract;

(6) they will each repose trust and confidence in each other, but of a different kind to that involved in fiduciary relationships;

(7) the contract in question will involve a high degree of communication, co-operation and predictable performance based on mutual trust and confidence, and expectations of loyalty;

(8) there may be a degree of significant investment by one part (or both in the venture. This significant investment may be, in some cases, more accurately described as substantial financial commitment; and

(9) exclusivity of the relationship may also be present.

2.131 It is important to note that the existence of a relational contract between parties does not necessarily mean that the court will automatically imply a duty of good faith. As the Court of Appeal in *Globe Motors v TRW Lucas*

108. [2019] EWHC 606 (QB). The 'relational contract' concept is not without criticism. In *UTB LLC v Sheffield United Ltd* [2019] EWHC 2322 (Ch), Fancourt J stated: 'there is a danger in using the term 'relational contract' that one is not clear about what exactly is meant by it. There is a great range of different types of contract that involve parties in long-term relationship of varying types, with different terms and varying degrees of detail and use of language, and to characterise them all as 'relational contracts' may be in one sense accurate and yet in other ways liable to mislead.'

Varity[109] stated, 'an implication of a duty of good faith will only be possible where the language of the contract, viewed against its context, permits it. It is thus not a reflection of a special rule of interpretation for [relational contracts]'.[110]

2.132 The court will seek to give effect to an express term in a commercial agreement that stipulates parties must exercise contractual rights and obligations in good faith. What exactly does 'good faith' entail? Perhaps this uncertainty is one reason preventing courts from fully embracing good faith. It has been said that 'the content of a duty of good faith is heavily conditioned by its context and the test of good faith is objective in that it depends on whether, in the particular context, the conduct would be regarded as commercially unacceptable by reasonable and honest people, and that its content is established through a process of construction of the contract'.[111]

Relevance in Hong Kong

2.133 The Hong Kong courts have yet to be afforded an opportunity to rule on the applicability of *Yam Seng*.[112] A number of uncertainties remain. For example, it remains to be seen if there will be further judicial guidance on how to recognise special contractual relationships. This would be beneficial because, in light of the features that have been identified, it is inevitable to conclude that all contracts hold some degree of relationality or could be deemed as relational.[113]

2.134 It has been observed that a 'good faith' obligation in a construction contract may encourage an arbitrator or judge called upon to construe the contract to be 'bold', that is, slightly more willing to give effect to the obvious purpose underlying the contract.[114] However, this is inevitably limited by the language of the agreement itself.[115]

2.135 Furthermore, it has also been said that the implication of the term 'good faith' into construction contracts is of little utility. In particular, a large

109. [2016] EWCA Civ 396.
110. *UTB LLC v Sheffield United Ltd* [2019] EWHC 2322 (Ch) at para. 202: 'It is self-evidently not all long-term contracts that involve an enduring but undefined, cooperative relationship between the parties that will, as a matter of law, involve an obligation of good faith.'
111. *Mid Essex Hospital Services NHS Trust v Compass Group UK* [2013] EWCA Civ 200.
112. That is not to say *Yam Seng* has not been discussed in Hong Kong at the highest judicial level. To the contrary, Justice Susan Kiefel of the High Court of Australia discussed 'Good Faith in Contractual Performance' at the the biennial Asia-Pacific Judicial Colloquium in 2015.
113. D. Campbell, 'Adam Smith and the Social Function of Agreement: *Walford v Miles* as a Relational Contract' (2017) 21 *Edinburgh Law Review* 376–404.
114. 'Does Good Faith Have Any Role in Construction Contracts', Pinsent Masons Lecture in Hong Kong on 22 November 2017 by Sir Rupert Jackson.
115. Ibid. See also *Arnold v Britton* [2015] UKSC 36.

number of individuals who had no involvement in the drafting of the contract will be required to operate in accordance with its provisions. In practical terms, they would likely rely on the express terms of the agreement only as it would be nonsensical to call their lawyers to determine the potential meaning of 'good faith' at every turn.[116]

2.136 How all these factors affect the operation of the NCE forms of contracts that are being more and more widely adopted in public works contracts in Hong Kong is yet to be seen.

116. Ibid.

3

Pre-contractual Documents, Communication, and Misrepresentation

Isaac Yung

Introduction

3.1 In the construction industry, the time taken by the parties to enter into a contract can sometimes be lengthy, involving the main contracts, the subcontracts, various pre-contractual documents and communications between the parties. The process may be protracted for a number of reasons; for example, preliminary investigations may need to be conducted or tender queries may need to be sought and answered; there may be one or multiple tenderer meetings; there may be alternative bids or designs or cost-saving designs involved. It can be expected that numerous discussions and meetings (by way of different media such as emails, teleconferences, in-person meetings, etc.) will be conducted before the parties formally enter into a contract.

3.2 When a dispute arises, it is not uncommon for parties to seek to introduce (usually voluminous) pre-contractual discussions or documents, contents of negotiations, and other extrinsic evidence to assist in the construction of the contract.[1] The drafting and wording of such documents and communications may sometimes be no less important than terms of the contract proper.

Letter of Intent

3.3 It is not uncommon for parties to issue and be issued with letters of intent during or after negotiations, especially in the construction industry. Depending on the wording and drafting of such a letter, a party may issue the letter without intending it to have any legal effect but merely to act as a form of reassurance to the other party; sometimes, the party issuing it may request the other party to proceed with necessary preparatory works in anticipation of entering into the contract; sometimes, the parties may

1. *Hyundai Engineering and Construction Co Ltd v Vigour Ltd* [2005] 3 HKLRD 723 at para. 41; *Konwall Construction Engineering Co Ltd v Strong Progress Ltd* [2013] 3 HKLRD 503. Such extrinsic evidence is subject to the parol evidence rule discussed in Chapter 2.

utilise the letter of intent as the contract between them pending the execution of a formal contract.

3.4 Thus, different parties may use letters of intent for different purposes. Ultimately, the parties will outline some of the most basic, fundamental terms of an agreement before they negotiate and settle the finer points and details. However, depending on how it is drafted, a letter of intent may contain all the elements of a binding contract. Consequently, it is not uncommon for the parties to subsequently dispute whether the letter of intent constitutes a binding contract, particularly when works have proceeded but no formal contract has been executed.

3.5 A common dispute is therefore whether the parties have intended the letter of intent to be a binding contract, in full or in part, or otherwise.

3.6 This can be resolved by an express provision in the letter of intent or a true construction of the letter of intent. For example, the inclusion of a 'subject to contract clause' may prevent a court from concluding that there was already a contract, although, as with many issues, each case will have to be decided on its own facts.[2]

3.7 It is important to be mindful that, when considering the nature of the agreement, the relationship between or past dealings of the parties will be considered. Generally, if the relationships or dealings were business-related rather than social or gratuitous, then the party who asserts that there was no legal effect to the agreement between the parties has a heavy onus to prove as such.[3] Furthermore, it is well-established that 'contractual intention is to be ascertained objectively. Evidence of the subjective intention of the parties is of limited value'.[4]

3.8 Therefore, if the language of the letter of intent does not expressly negate the parties' intention to contract, it is open to the court to hold parties bound by the document.[5]

3.9 A letter of intent can still have contractual or other effect even if the parties contemplate that the letter is to be superseded by a later, more formal, contractual document.[6]

3.10 Depending on the wording used in a letter of intent, it may be drafted in such a way that certain terms of it will have contractual force, while

2. Once a 'subject to contract' qualification is introduced into negotiations, it will only cease to apply if the parties expressly or by necessary implication agree that it should be expunged: *Cohen v Nessdale Ltd* [1982] 2 All ER 97 (CA).
3. *Cable & Wireless (Hong Kong) Ltd Staff Association v ng Kong Telecom International Ltd* [2001] 2 HKLRD 809 at para. 30, citing *Edwards v Skyways Ltd* [1964] 1 WLR 349; [1964] 1 All ER 494 with approval.
4. *Best Star Holdings Ltd v Lam Chun Hing Others* [2012] HKCFI 211 at para. 116.
5. *Associated British Ports v Ferryways* [2008] EWCA Civ 189.
6. *Diamond Build Ltd v Clapham Park Homes Ltd* [2008] EWHC 1439 (TCC).

other terms may not. There can also be *quantum meruit*[7] in the absence of contract. In *British Steel Corporation v Cleveland Bridge & Engineering Co Ltd*,[8] as requested, works had begun before all elements of the contract had been agreed and no contract was later entered into.

Letters of Comfort

3.11 A letter of comfort is a tool of commerce developed to provide an alternative to guarantee or surety.[9] For example, a parent company may be unwilling to give a more conventional form of security for its subsidiary's liabilities, or party who deals with a subsidiary may seek assurance from the parent company concerning the liabilities undertaken by its subsidiary. Furthermore, the parent company may not wish to incur legal liability, or may want to protect its own credit rating, or wants to avoid showing a contingent liability on its balance sheet.[10]

3.12 A typical example in the field of construction occurs when a creditor makes a loan to the subsidiary. While the parent company may refuse to provide an official guarantee, it may decide to provide the creditor with a statement assuring the subsidiary's capacity to meet the necessary obligations. Such an assurance, usually by way of letter, is often referred to as a letter of comfort.

3.13 If the subsidiary defaults on the loan, the creditor may consider pursuing the parent company to meet the subsidiary's obligations. Whether or not the creditor is successful in seeking relief against the parent company turns on whether the letter of comfort was intended to create an enforceable contractual relationship between the creditor and the parent company.

3.14 In *Kleinwort Benson Ltd v Malaysia Mining Corporation*,[11] the plaintiff bank made a loan to the defendant's subsidiary. The defendant provided two 'letters of comfort', each stated 'it is our policy to ensure that the business of [the subsidiary] is at all times in a position to meet its liabilities to you under the above arrangements'.

3.15 The defendant's subsidiary defaulted on the loan and the plaintiff bank sought to recover from the parent defendant company on the basis that

7. *Quantum meruit* is a category of remedy with restitutionary effect. It is available when a party has provided a benefit but for some reason cannot obtain payment under a contract. In such circumstances, that party may recover the reasonable value of the benefit so provided. It means 'the amount he deserves' or 'what the job is worth'. One common example of *quantum meruit* is where no price is stated for works carried out within an existing contract and the employer is obliged to pay a reasonable sum.
8. [1984] 1 All ER 504.
9. *Bouygues SA v Shanghai Links Executive Community Ltd* [1998] 2 HKLRD 479 at para. 28.
10. *Bouygues SA v Shanghai Links Executive Community Ltd* [1998] 2 HKLRD 479 at para. 28.
11. [1989] 1 All ER 785; [1989] 1 WLR 379.

the letter of comfort constituted a contractual guarantee. At trial, the plaintiff bank succeeded when the court held that the parent company had failed to rebut the presumption against contractual intention in commercial agreements.[12] The parent company appealed.

3.16 The English Court of Appeal held that the material clause was merely a statement of present fact of the intentions of the parent defendant company and not a promise as to its future conduct. Therefore, the letter created no contractual obligations between the plaintiff bank and the parent defendant company.

Case illustrations

3.17 Nonetheless, the use of letters of intent or sometimes letters of comfort, particularly in the construction industry, is understandable. Prior to the signing of the contract, there are numerous issues to be resolved and there is often immense pressure to commence works as soon as possible as deliverables are often on a tight schedule.

3.18 One would think that the existence of a contract itself would never be the subject of dispute in construction litigation. Yet, this is not necessarily the case.

3.19 In *British Steel Corporation v Cleveland Bridge*,[13] the subcontractor successfully tendered for the fabrication of steel works in the construction of a building. The contractor sent a letter of intent to the subcontractor which recorded the contractor' intention to enter into a contract with the subcontractor, proposed that the subcontract be on the contractor's standard form, and requested the subcontractor to commence works immediately 'pending the preparation and issuing to you of the official form of subcontract'.

3.20 Even though there were extensive discussions on a number of issues, the subcontractor proceeded to manufacture and deliver the steel nodes. However, there was delay in delivering one steel node. The contractor refused to pay for the steel nodes.

3.21 Although Goff J initially discussed the possibility that the letters of intent could give rise to two different types of contract, his Lordship ultimately rejected both on the basis that the letters of intent in question applied 'pending a formal subcontract the terms of which were still in a state of negotiation'.

12. [1988] 1 All ER 714; [1988] 1 WLR 799.
13. [1984] 1 All ER 504.

3.22 Similarly, in *Four Sea Union (Holdings) Ltd v Hong Kong & Macau Scent On Engineering & Construction Ltd*,[14] both parties to the dispute were construction companies. The defendant was a contractor on the Hong Kong Government List of Contractors for Public Works, whereas the plaintiff was not. There was an arrangement between the plaintiff and the defendant, and thereafter the plaintiff submitted a tender to the government for works and was successful. The original plan was that the plaintiff would carry out the works and the defendant would receive 4% of the contract payments as management fee. The plaintiff commenced works on 1 March 2001, but quickly ceased at the end of May as neither parties were able to agree to the terms upon which the contract between them should be signed.

3.23 On the evidence, as well as the plaintiff's own pleadings, the court ruled that there was no binding agreement between the parties.

Tender Documents[15]

3.24 Main contractors in construction projects often acquire such works through a tendering process. It is important to have a good understanding of the legal principles before discussing the actual documents involved in the tendering process.

3.25 There is sometimes a general but incorrect presumption that tenders are and can only be invitations to treat, or otherwise known as invitations to other parties to make an offer.[16] Such a presumption will usually be displaced when the surrounding circumstances and the words used in the invitation for parties to make offers could be reasonably interpreted as the party calling for tenders intended as offers.

3.26 When the tender is accepted by the inviting party, a contract is concluded. However, a prior collateral contract may arise before the conclusion of the principal contract in the following manner—there is an implied obligation on the party inviting the tender to consider all confirming tenders according to the invitation to tender, thereby providing consideration for a collateral contract, i.e. the 'process' contract, brought into being upon the submission of a tender.[17] This is a natural consequence of the tenderer's own obligation to be bound by the conditions of tendering.

---

14. [2003] 1 HKLRD 653.
15. Information obtained from 'Reference Material on Section of Contractors' by the Construction Industry Council, dated December 2019.
16. *Spencer v Harding* (1870) LR 5 CP 561. Such an invitation is an invitation to others to make an offer and the invitation in itself is not an offer that can be accepted into forming a contract.
17. *City University of Hong Kong v Blue Cross (Asia-Pacific) Insurance Ltd* [2001] 1 HKC 463.

3.27 In *Pioneer Catering Equipment & Engineering Ltd v Secretary for Justice*,[18] Pioneer Catering specialised in the supply and installation of catering equipment and was on the list of Approved Suppliers of Materials Specialist Contractors for Public Works (the List) that was maintained by the Architectural Services Department (ASD). With reference to three separate construction contracts, all the contractors on the List were invited to submit tenders. Pioneer Catering responded to all three invitations by submitting three separate tenders, two of which were the tender.

3.28 There was no dispute that the government had not considered Pioneer Catering's three tenders at all, which was the construction company's chief complaint.

3.29 The issue was whether the government was entitled *not* to consider the tenders in the circumstances. This was dependent on the terms of Conditions of Tender for each of the invitations. As it turned out, the second and third invitations contained a 'Suspension Clause'—its effect was that by the tender closing date, if the tenderer was under suspension from tendering for public works, his tender would not be considered unless the suspension was lifted within 40 days from and including the tender closing date.

3.30 At the time of submitting the tenders, Pioneer Catering was in fact suspended and its suspension was never lifted. Furthermore, the second and third invitations to tender contained the Suspension Clause. While the first invitation did not contain such a clause, the court found it equitable to imply such a clause.

3.31 As the construction company was bound by the conditions of the tender, its failure to adhere to those conditions entitled the government to not consider any of its tenders.

Form of tendering

3.32 There are typically two types of tendering—open tendering and selective tendering.

3.33 In open tendering, a public announcement for invitation to tender is made, typically in a local newspaper or on the company's website. Interested contractors who meet the prescribed requirements in the announcement may submit a tender.

3.34 In selective tendering, only contractors that meet a pre-qualification process are invited to submit a tender. During the pre-qualification assessment, the contractor may be asked to show records relating to its

18. [2004] 3 HKC 357.

qualifications, finances, and technical expertise, and to identify any conflicts of interests.

3.35 Once potential tenderers have been identified, whether through open or selective tendering, the employer typically provides a compilation of documents (i.e. tender documents) to such tenderers. Tender documents in construction projects typically include the following:

1. conditions of tender
2. form of tender
3. articles of agreement
4. general conditions of contract
5. special conditions of contract
6. specifications
7. drawings
8. technical submissions
9. bills of quantities or schedule of rates (as may be the case)
10. other standard documents incorporated by the above

Conditions of tender

3.36 The Conditions of Tender provide the general framework of which the tenderer should be aware of when preparing their tender. Common information includes the name and title of the project, how the tender should be completed and returned, place and date for return of tenders, and documents and information to be provided with the tender.

Form of tender

3.37 A potential tenderer will first receive an invitation to submit a tender. The form of tender is then submitted by the tenderer. Typically, the form of tender will incorporate the following:

1. the name of the employer to whom/which the offer will be made
2. the price of the works, which should be the same as other parts of the tender documents
3. the validity period of the offer
4. warranties that will be provided outside the contract, if any
5. a disclaimer by the employer stating that there is no obligation to accept the lowest or any tender returned

3.38 It is often the case that the form of tender must be signed by an authorised person on behalf of the tenderer.

Articles of agreement

3.39 The Articles of Agreement set out the agreement in substance and the signatories. These define the parties to the contract and its contents.

General and special conditions of the contract

3.40 The General Conditions of the Contract will typically simply be one of the standard forms of contract that is widely available in the market.

3.41 As most construction projects will use such a standard form contract, Special Conditions of the Contract designed for the particular construction project will also be inserted and must be read in conjunction with the general conditions. Usually, special conditions are drafted to suit the preferences of the employer. These may include:

1. the tenderer's contractual/statutory obligations
2. the use of materials which are new, free from defects and of good quality
3. variations of works
4. contract bills
5. insurance requirements
6. extension of time
7. liquidated damages

Specifications

3.42 In general, specifications refer to the information describing the type and quality of materials and workmanship needed to complete the project. Specifications may be further divided into different parts. These are typically the preliminaries, the general technical specification and the particular technical specification.

3.43 Preliminaries will list the general requirements that will be applicable across the whole project.

3.44 General technical specifications are usually a generic set of specifications and it is not uncommon to use publicly available technical specifications.

3.45 Particular technical specifications are specifications that are specific to the project at hand. Special technical requirements or materials needed for the completion of the project will be included.

Drawings

3.46 Design drawings are prepared by architects and/or engineers. It is important to examine the drawings in conjunction with the technical specifications to have a full grasp of the project and the works needed to be done.

Technical submissions

3.47 The tenderer is required to provide submissions on technical resources and technical proposals which will eventually form part of the contract. Technical submissions are a critical part of the tender usually subjected to critical assessment from the employer.

Bills of quantities or schedule rates

3.48 Bills of quantities (BQ) or schedule of rates (SoR) refer to the pricing of the tender documents. If a BQ is tendered, all items in the bills must be priced.

Case illustration

3.49 Each of the documents above forms an essential element of the contract and all of them, as parts of the contract, are to be read together as one entire agreement.

3.50 The importance of tender documents cannot be overstated. In particular, the tenderer must be familiar with its own documents. In *Fai Tak Engineering Ltd v Sui Chong Construction & Engineering Co Ltd*,[19] Fai Tak commenced proceedings to claim a sum it alleged was due and owing from Sui Chong under their agreement. However, Sui Chong applied to stay proceedings on the ground that the parties had agreed to submit to arbitration any dispute or difference arising under the agreement.

3.51 Mimmie Chan DCJ stated in unequivocal terms that, Fai Tak having submitted the tender expressed to be in accordance with the tender documents and conditions, and having agreed to use and be bound by the Standard Form of Domestic Subcontract, it was not open to Fai Tak to say that it had not read the detailed terms and conditions of the tender documents or the Standard Form of Subcontract or the arbitration clause contained in the Standard Form and that for such reason it should not be bound thereby.[20]

---

19. [2009] HKDC 1854.
20. *Fai Tak Engineering Ltd v Sui Chong Construction & Engineering Co Ltd* [2009] HKDC 1854 at para. 45.

Pre-contractual Communications

3.52 Most pre-contractual communication can generally be distilled into one word—negotiation. This is unsurprising as the ultimate goal of most, if not all, communication between the parties is to shape and form the agreement in each party's respective favour.

3.53 A common question that arises in contractual disputes is the extent of relevance of the communications between parties. In this day and age, pre-contractual communication is less likely to include parties' discussions at the negotiation table. Pre-contractual communication could include oral discussions, however, along with emails and letter correspondences.

3.54 Whether pre-contractual communication is admissible as evidence for the purpose of interpreting the agreement between the parties is subject to the parol evidence rule discussed in Chapter 2.

Misrepresentation

3.55 As construction projects become increasingly complex, parties to construction contracts are likely to undertake numerous rounds of negotiations before a finalised agreement is drafted. In general, oral or written statements made in the course of such negotiations can be broadly classified as 'terms' or 'representations'.

3.56 Statements are terms if parties intended them to form part of the agreement. In contrast, if statements are made only with the intention of inducing the other party to conclude the agreement, those statements are representations. A representation may be made by one party to the other before entering into the contract in regard to some existing fact or past event.

3.57 In its simplest form, misrepresentation occurs when a party makes a statement of fact, which is not true, with the intention of inducing the other party to conclude the contract, and the other party is so induced.

3.58 A third kind of pre-contractual statement that is neither a term nor representation is known as a mere 'puff'. Puffs are statements which could not reasonably be understood as having been intended to produce any legal consequences. An operative element of misrepresentation is that the misrepresentor has made a statement of fact which is not true, and this must be distinguished from a statement that is 'mere puff'.

3.59 A common and everyday example of mere puffs would be some vague statements made, for example, in advertising, such as "this makes you feel beautiful".

3.60 In *Chan Yeuk Yu and Another v Church Body of the Hong Kong Sheng Kung Hui and Another*,[21] the plaintiffs, *inter alia*, sought to rescind the agreement they had entered into for the purchase of an apartment. The plaintiffs advanced a number of grounds, one of which claimed that they had been induced into the agreement by representations contained in the sales brochure presented by the defendants that the apartment would be 'regal surroundings for the select few'.

3.61 The judge determined that, in the context of the case, i.e., where the wording of 'regal surroundings for the select few' appeared on a page of a glossy and colour sales brochure, it was no more than 'mere puff' or a 'sales pitch'. The judge further held that that was vague promotional language, which, in any event, was not false.

3.62 Whether a statement is a term or a representation is to be determined by the parties' objectively established intention.[22] For example, if the parties have agreed that a particular statement is a term or a representation, that is the end of the matter.

3.63 However, it is more likely the case that these intentions have not been made clear. As a result, the circumstances of each case must be examined to determine what the objective intention of each party is.

3.64 Distinguishing between a term and a representation is important, as a breach of the former gives rise to a cause of action based on contract, the latter based on misrepresentation.

Determining the Intention of the Parties

Invitation to verify

3.65 Where a party makes a statement and suggests that the other party verify it for themselves, it is likely that the statement was intended to be a representation rather than a term.[23]

Invitation not to verify

3.66 In contrast, where a statement is made and the other party is encouraged not to confirm its veracity, it is likely that the statement was intended to be a term rather than a representation.[24]

21. [2001] 1 HKC 621.
22. *Oscar Chess Ltd Williams* [1957] 1 All ER 325; [1957] 1 WLR 370.
23. *Ecay v Godfrey* (1947) 80 L1 L Rep 286.
24. *Schawel v Reade* [1913] 2 IR 81; 46 ILT 281.

Timing of the statement

3.67 The passage of time between a statement being made (or repeated) and the conclusion of the agreement is a factor the court will consider. In general, the longer the interval, the greater the presumption that the parties did not intend the statement to have contractual effect in relation to a subsequent deal.[25]

Declaration of importance

3.68 A party who declares that a statement that has been made to him is of importance to him will likely have intended for the statement to constitute a term of the contract.

Relative expertise of parties

3.69 Where a party making a statement possesses less expertise or special knowledge concerning the statement's subject matter than the party to whom the statement is addressed, it is less likely that the statement was intended to be a contractual term.

Reduced to writing

3.70 As discussed in Chapter 2, the parol evidence rule will likely apply to an agreement that has been reduced into writing. Generally speaking, statements which are left out of the written agreement are likely not to be regarded as terms.

'Entire contract/agreement' clauses

3.71 One of the more effective methods of preventing another party to an agreement from claiming terms or representations arising out of negotiations is to draft a comprehensive and clear entire contract clause. Such clauses are designed to make it clear that the agreement constitutes the entirety of the agreement between the parties in relation to the subject matter and will supersede and replace any other agreements, conditions, or representations (oral or written), whether express or implied. If drafted properly, such a clause will likely succeed in preventing a party arguing that a pre-contractual statement was intended by the parties to constitute a term of the agreement.

25. *Inntrepreneur Pub Co (GL) v East Crown Ltd* [2000] 2 Lloyd's Rep 611 at 615; *Schawel v Reade* [1913] 2 IR 81; 46 ILT 281.

Types of Pre-contractual Representations

Misrepresentation of opinion

3.72 In general, only misrepresentation of fact is actionable. Misrepresentation of opinion or future intention is not, unless a statement of opinion is published as a statement of fact or a statement of future intention is not honestly meant.[26]

Misrepresentation by conduct

3.73 As in the case of a written or oral misrepresentation, a person may be liable for misrepresentation by conduct if such conduct was intended to convey factual information.

3.74 In *Green Park Properties Ltd v Dorku Ltd*,[27] the defendant was the registered owner of a property that was partitioned into Portions A and B. After the second inspection of the property, the purchaser plaintiff raised a question concerning the size and position of two columns within Portion A. The estate agent showed a copy of the tenancy plan, which indicated that a walled yard was part of Portion A. The sale and purchase agreement was shortly concluded thereafter, but subsequently it was discovered that the walled yard in Portion A was actually part of the building's common area and that it was not included in the sale. The plaintiff sought to rescind the provisional agreement for sale and purchase.

3.75 The judge found that there was misrepresentation by conduct, first by showing the property to the plaintiff and second by showing the tenancy plan to the plaintiff. The appellate court agreed.

3.76 The appellate court specifically rejected the argument that there had to be an intention on that part of the representor to mislead the representee. In other words, it is sufficient that the representation by conduct was objectively misleading as to a fact which induced the representee to conclude the contract.[28]

Misrepresentation of intention

3.77 In general, a statement of future intentions is not usually considered to be a statement of existing fact. However, a statement regarding doing

26. *Top One International (China) Property Group Co Ltd and Another v Top One Property Group Ltd and Others* [2011] HKCFI 593 at para. 24.
27. [2000] 4 HKC 538; [2001] 1 HKLRD 139.
28. Ibid., at para. 7.

or abstaining from doing something may, under certain circumstances, amount to a representation of existing fact.[29]

3.78 To put it another way, if the court is satisfied that the person who makes the forecast implies that he now believes that his prediction will come true or that he has the means of bringing to pass, it would be a representation which is actionable.[30]

Misrepresentation of law

3.79 The original rule in common law was that a misrepresentation of law was not actionable, which meant that there could be no claim for rescission of the contract or an action for damages. This correctness of this rule was brought into doubt with the House of Lords decision in *Kleinwort Benson Ltd v Lincoln City Council*,[31] where it was ruled for the first time that money paid as a result of a mistake of law could be reclaimed by the mistaken party.

3.80 It was further held in *Pankhania v Hackney LBC*[32] that the 'misrepresentation of law' rule is no longer good law. Hence, the distinction between statements of law and statements of fact may no longer be maintainable. In other words, a misstatement on law may now amount to misrepresentation.

Types of Misrepresentation

3.81 The innocent party that has been subjected to misrepresentation can claim remedies depending on the type of misrepresentation –fraudulent, negligent, or innocent.

Fraudulent misrepresentation

3.82 A statement made with the knowledge of its falsity, or without belief in its truth, or made recklessly not caring whether it is true or false, is considered a fraudulent misrepresentation.[33]

3.83 A claim of fraudulent misrepresentation is extremely serious and the burden to prove it is heavy.

---

29. *Mak's Construction Co Ltd v Sun Fook Kong (Civil) Ltd* [2002] HKCFI 568 at para. 31. Ma J (as he then was) further referred to *British Airways Board v Taylor* [1976] 1 WLR 13, where Lord Wilberforce stated that 'everyone is familiar with the proposition that a statement of intention may itself be a statement of fact and so capable of being true or false' (at 17D-E).
30. *Kwai Tak Ming v K.S. Capital One Ltd and Others* [2017] 4 HKLRD 19 at para. 72.
31. [1999] 2 AC 349.
32. [2002] EWHC 2441 (Ch).
33. *Derry v Peek* (1881) 14 App Cas 337.

3.84 One such case is *Sear v Kingfisher Builders*.[34] Mr Chudley, a partner of Kingfisher Builders, in an attempt to persuade that Kingfisher Builders was the right company to renovate and extend Mr Sear's house, suggested that Mr Sear speak to Mrs Whale, who he suggested was a happy customer of Kingfisher Builders.

3.85 Unbeknownst to Mr Sear, Mrs Whale was a partner in the Kingfisher Builders business, which she failed to disclose. Furthermore, she also failed to disclose that she was in a relationship with Mr Chudley, but deliberately gave the impression that she was an independent third party for whom Kingfisher Business had carried out work. Finally, she also failed to disclose that Mr Chudley had a conviction for fraud and had been made bankrupt.

3.86 The judge held that her failure to disclose those matters amounted to fraudulent misrepresentation.[35]

3.87 The court found that Mrs Whale acted fraudulently by participating in the charade and giving the appearance of being an independent third party. It further held that the misrepresentation was made with the intention that it be relied upon, as it was. Therefore, Mrs Whale was liable for fraudulent misrepresentation.[36]

3.88 The court ordered Mrs Whale to pay Mr Sear £376,432.81 as damages for fraudulent misrepresentation.[37]

3.89 In *The Hong Kong Housing Authority v Hsin Yieh Architects & Associates Ltd and Others*,[38] the Housing Authority had, by way of contract, engaged the 3rd defendant (B+B Construction) to design and construct the piling and pile cap foundations for six 41-storey Concord-style blocks and two schools at Tin Shui Wai.

3.90 The Housing Authority eventually discovered short piling at Blocks 1 and 2, which was in breach of the parties' contract.

3.91 The court needed to determine whether personnel of B+B had made fraudulent or deceitful misrepresentations in the as-built piling records and other reports submitted to the Housing Authority, intending that the latter should act on them and causing loss and damage when the Housing Authority did so act.

3.92 Under cross-examination, even B+B's piling and engineering expert accepted that the inaccuracies in the as-built piling records could not be attributed to mere inadvertence. As such, the court held that such

34. (No 3) [2013] EWHC 21 (TCC).
35. Ibid., at para. 7.
36. Ibid., at para. 7.
37. (No. 3) [2013] EWHC 21 (TCC).
38. [2005] HKCFI 741.

records were deliberately certified by B+B's on-site staff to mislead the Housing Authority into believing that all was well with the Block 1 and 2 foundations.[39]

Negligent misrepresentation

3.93 An untrue representation made carelessly, or without reasonable grounds for believing it to be true, is known as a negligent misrepresentation.[40]

Innocent misrepresentation

3.94 A misrepresentation which is neither fraudulent nor negligent is known as an innocent misrepresentation. At common law, a victim of innocent misrepresentation did not have an action for damages. However, this has been ameliorated by the Misrepresentation Ordinance (Cap 284) as discussed below.[41]

Remedies for Misrepresentation

Rescission

3.95 An innocent contracting party who has been the victim of any type of misrepresentation may be entitled to rescind the contract.

3.96 Rescission is a powerful remedy as it allows the innocent contracting party to terminate the contract at the point of inception. Such an act places the parties in the position as if the contract had never been entered into.

3.97 Rescission is only effective upon communication to the other party, although, in practice, parties tend to seek an order from the court for rescission. In circumstances where the misrepresentor cannot be located, it is sufficient that the innocent party show that reasonable steps have been taken to rescind the contract.

3.98 As the remedy places the parties in the position as if the contract had not existed, the representee must also return, or offer to return, any consideration under the agreement as would be necessary to affect a restoration of the status prior to the contract.

3.99 Hence in *Joytex Development Ltd v Super Homes Ltd*,[42] after the court held there was misrepresentation involved in the sale of a flat, it ordered that

39. Ibid., at para. 203.
40. Hugh Beale, *Chitty on Contracts*, 33rd ed. (Sweet & Maxwell, 2020), at para. 7-076.
41. It should be noted that section 3(1) of the Misrepresentation Ordinance does not per se give a victim a right to claim damages, but merely grants the court discretion to grant damages to the victim in lieu of rescinding the contract.
42. [2018] HKCFI 2286.

the plaintiff was entitled to repayment of the purchase price of the flat with interest and, upon such repayment, the defendant would be entitled to have the flat conveyed back to it.

Bars to rescission

3.100 Certain factors may bar the innocent party from rescinding the contract for misrepresentation.

3.101 For example, if the innocent party makes express statements or takes certain actions that affirm the contract, the right to rescission is lost.[43] A lapse of time after discovering the misrepresentation may be evidence of affirming the contract.[44] Under usual circumstances, there can be no affirmation if the innocent party is unaware of the misrepresentation in the first place and therefore the right to rescind is preserved.

3.102 Once the innocent party is aware of the misrepresentation, prompt action should be taken, especially if he intends to exercise the right to rescission. In particular, his wish to rescind should be made known to the misrepresentor in reasonable time, as a lengthy time lapse from the discovery of the misrepresentation to the time of taking action to rescind the contract may be sufficient to bar this right.[45]

3.103 It is also a bar to rescission if and when a *bona fide* third party acquires for value an interest in the contract's subject matter.

3.104 Finally, it may be a bar to rescission if circumstances have developed such that parties' original positions simply cannot be restored.[46]

3.105 However, it has been suggested by authoritative authors that a more flexible approach should be adopted, for example granting a *quantum meruit* to the misrepresentee where he discovers that an innocent misrepresentation has been made only after he has performed some of the services required of him.[47]

3.106 Finally, prior to the enactment of the Misrepresentation Ordinance (Cap 284), there were two further bars to rescission for non-fraudulent misrepresentation—if the misrepresentation had become a contractual term

---

43. *Seddon v North Eastern Sal Co* [1905] 1 Ch 326; [1904–07] All ER Rep 817.
44. *Clough v London and North Western Railway Co* (1871) L.R. 7 Exch 26.
45. In *Leaf v International Galleries* [1950] 2 KB 86; [1950] All ER 693, the plaintiff purchased a painting from the defendant because it was allegedly painted by a famous English artist. It turned out that this was not correct. However, the plaintiff only intimated his intention to rescind the agreement of purchase five years after the date of purchase. The Court of Appeal (having affirmed the first instance judgment) did not allow rescission.
46. *Clarke v Dickson* (1858) EB & E; 120 ER 463.
47. Huge Beale, *Chitty on Contracts*, 33rd ed. (Sweet & Maxwell, 2020), at [7-129]. In *Parkwell Commercial Ltd v Sweet View Properties* [2000] HKCFI 1482 at para. 7, Chung J appears to accept that the modern approach to rescission can be flexible.

or if the contract had been performed. Section 2 of the Misrepresentation Ordinance (Cap 284) states the following:

2. Removal of certain bars to rescission for innocent misrepresentation

Where a person has entered into a contract after a misrepresentation has been made to him, and—

(a) the misrepresentation has become a term of the contract; or

(b) the contract has been performed,

or both, then, if otherwise he would be entitled to rescind the contract without alleging fraud, he shall be so entitled, subject to the provisions of this Ordinance, notwithstanding the matters mentioned in paragraphs (a) and (b).

Damages

3.107 A victim of fraudulent misrepresentation is entitled to rescind the contract (as discussed above), claim damages or both.

3.108 Damages in a case of fraudulent misrepresentation is measured as if the misrepresentations had not been made with the objective of putting the plaintiff, as far as possible, into the same position financially as if he had not entered into the contract at all.[48] This is in contrast with the typical measure of damages for a breach of contract, which is to place the innocent party in the position as if the representation were true.

3.109 In addition, damages awards can include all actual damages directly flowing from (i.e. caused by) entering into the contract, and are not limited to those which are reasonably foreseeable (though the damages must not be too remote, i.e. not of a type which would foreseeably flow from the misrepresentation).[49]

Misrepresentation Ordinance (Cap 284)

3.110 The purpose of the Misrepresentation Ordinance (Cap 284) is to reform the availability of rescission and damages (in particular for negligent or innocent misrepresentation) as remedies for misrepresentation.

3.111 Section 3 of the Misrepresentation Ordinance (Cap 284) is as follows:

3. Damages for misrepresentation

48. Per Liu JA at para. 27 in *Polaroid Far East Ltd v Bel Trade Co Ltd and Others* [990] HKCA 339, citing *Doyle v Olby (Ironmongers) Ltd* [1969] 2 QB 158 at 171 E–F with approval.

49. Per Ribeiro JA (as he then was) at para. 27 in *Dr Andrew Kee-Suan Koh v Dr Vincent Kay-Lo Ip* [2000] HKCA 506, citing *Smith New Court Securities Ltd v Citibank NA* [1997] AC 254 and *Doyle v Olby (Ironmongers) Ltd* [1969] 2 QB 158 with approval.

(1) Where a person has entered into a contract after a misrepresentation has been made to him by another party thereto and as a result thereof he has suffered loss, then, if the person making the misrepresentation would be liable to damages in respect thereof had the misrepresentation been made fraudulently, that person shall be so liable notwithstanding that the misrepresentation was not made fraudulently, unless he proves that he had reasonable grounds to believe and did believe up to the time the contract was made that the facts represented were true.

(2) Where a person has entered into a contract after a misrepresentation has been made to him otherwise than fraudulently, and he would be entitled, by reason of the misrepresentation, to rescind the contract, then, if it is claimed, in any proceedings arising out of the contract, that the contract ought to be or has been rescinded the court or arbitrator may declare the contract subsisting and award damages in lieu of rescission, if of opinion that it would be equitable to do so, having regard to the nature of the misrepresentation and the loss that would be caused by it if the contract were upheld, as well as to the loss that rescission would cause to the other party.

(3) . . .

3.112 Section 3(1) of the Misrepresentation Ordinance grants great assistance to a victim of non-fraudulent misrepresentation seeking damages because he would be entitled to such damages as if the representation had been fraudulent, unless the representor can prove that he had reasonable grounds to believe and did believe at the time of executing the contract that the facts represented were true.

3.113 Therefore, instead of the victim proving that the representor had *no* reasonable grounds to believe in the facts represented, the onus shifts to the representor to show that he *did* have reasonable grounds to believe in the facts that were represented.

3.114 In *Long Year Developments Ltd v Tse Fuk Man Norman & Ors (Ho Shiu Kwan Tony & Anor, Third Parties)*,[50] the third parties (i.e. Mr Ho and Madam Chan) contracted to sell a flat to the defendants (Mr Tse and Madam Yu). A car park, which was uncovered and difficult to manoeuvre a car in, was part of the sale and purchase of the flat. However, the third parties had informed the defendants that the car park was in fact the adjacent one, which was covered and easy to park in. The defendants believed in the representations of Mr Ho and Madam Chan. Thereafter, the defendants agreed to sub-sell the flat to the plaintiff.

3.115 When the truth came out, both sale and purchase agreements were rescinded. However, the plaintiff commenced proceedings against the defendants, who also commenced proceedings against the third parties.

50. [1991] 2 HKC 393.

3.116 The judge held that Madam Chan held the authority to deal with everything on behalf of Mr Ho and that she had believed throughout that the covered carpark was the carpark belonging to the third parties. Therefore, she was not guilty of fraudulent misrepresentation.[51]

3.117 However, addressing section 3(1) of the Misrepresentation Ordinance, the judge held that Madam Chan did not have reasonable grounds to hold such a belief because the basis of such belief was simply observing her tenant parking his car at the covered space on a single occasion and, furthermore, the matter could have been easily ascertained and verified from the title documents.

3.118 The judge finally held that the measure of damages arising from section 3(1) of the Misrepresentation Ordinance would be the same as for tortious deceit, i.e. damages would be awarded on the basis that the plaintiff is to be put in the position he would have been in had the representation not been made.

3.119 In contrast, section 3(2) of the Misrepresentation Ordinance empowers the court to substitute damages 'in lieu of rescission, if . . . it would be equitable to do so, having regard to the nature of the misrepresentation and the loss that would be caused by it if the contract were upheld, as well as to the loss that rescission would cause to the other party'.

3.120 The section makes it clear that it is applicable to a misrepresentation that has been made 'otherwise than fraudulently', meaning it is inapplicable to fraudulent misrepresentation and applies only to negligent and innocent misrepresentation. In other words, the court may not grant damages in lieu of rescission if the issue is fraudulent misrepresentation.

3.121 In *William Sindall Plc v Cambridgeshire County Council*,[52] Sindall had purchased land from the government for the purpose of developing it upon the council's representation that there were no easements. Two events occurred after completion of the sale. First, it was discovered that there was a private sewer from 20 years earlier and this would inevitably reduce the amount of development that could be conducted. Second, the market crashed and the value of the land plummeted. Sindall sued seeking rescission for misrepresentation and common mistake but was ultimately unsuccessful.

3.122 In *obiter*, Lord Hoffman considered that it would cost £18,000 to divert the sewers which would thereafter unlikely interfere in any serious manner with the development or re-sale of the property. This was of relatively minor importance compared to the impact on the city council, which

51. Ibid., at para. 50.
52. [1993] EWCA Civ 14; [1994] 1 WLR 1016.

would be required to return about £8.0 million in purchase price and interest in exchange for land worth less than £2.0 million.

3.123 Due to this gross disparity between the loss which would be caused to Sindall by the misrepresentation and the loss which would be caused to Cambridgeshire by rescission, his Lordship opined that he would have awarded damages in lieu of recession.

3.124 In contrast, if damages are unlikely to adequately compensate for what the representee had bargained for, it is less likely that the court will exercise its discretion pursuant to section 3(2).

3.125 In *Balchita Ltd v Kam Yuck Investment Co Ltd*,[53] Kempster J needed to decide whether to grant an order for damages in lieu of rescission under section 3(2). Balchita had agreed to purchase from Kam Yuck some ground floor shop units. The advertising brochures indicated that the ground floor of the shops was level with the adjacent street. As it turned out, the shops were beneath the level of the adjacent street.

3.126 Kempster J referred to what was said by Tindal CJ in *Flight v Booth*:[54] 'where the misdescription, although not proceeding from fraud, is in a material and a substantial point, so far affecting the subject matter of the contract that it may reasonably be supposed that, but for such misdescription, the purchaser might never have entered into the contract at all'. Balchita's claim to rescind the agreements for the purchase and sale of the shops and the recovery of the purchase price was allowed.

3.127 Similar sentiments were expressed by the Hong Kong Court of Appeal in *Green Park Properties Ltd v Dorku Ltd*.[55] Le Pichon JA, whom Rogers VP and Stock JA agreed,[56] was not persuaded that the misrepresentation was insubstantial and related to only 72 square feet of the overall size of the property, which was 2000 square feet, because what mattered was 'not the diminution in the overall area of the subject-matter of the sale but the importance of the yard to the owner of portion A. If the yard had been included, the owner should have exclusive control over access to the property from the lane and this was also an important consideration so far as security is concerned'.

3.128 Le Pichon JA also agreed with the trial judge's observations that the area would be more valuable to the owner if he could use it exclusively and not share it with others in the same building as there would be no restrictions.

53. [1983] HKCFI 170; [1983] 2 HKC 333.
54. (1834) 131 ER 1160. The case considered the issue of title defects and whether or not a misdescription of a property gave the purchaser the right to rescind the contract, notwithstanding the contractual clauses as drafted.
55. [2000] 4 HKC 538; [2001] 1 HKLRD 139. See facts of the case in para. 3-0045 above.
56. Le Pichon JA also identified the misrepresentation as being incapable of being remedied, which was also distinguishable with *William Sindall*.

For example, he would be at liberty to erect an awning or a more permanent cover to render the yard weather-proof, which would not be possible if it were a common area of the building.

Non-Reliance Clauses and Entire-Agreement Clauses

3.129 There are two clauses typically used to limit liability for misrepresentation: 'entire agreement' clauses[57] and 'non-reliance clauses'. Depending on the precise wording and proper construction of these clauses, if they effectively seek to limit liability of the parties they will only be effective if they are held to be reasonable pursuant to the Control of Exemption Clauses Ordinance (Cap 71) (CECO).

Entire agreement clause

3.130 In *Inntrepreneur Pub Co (GL) v East Crown Ltd,*[58] Lightman J analysed the purpose and rationale behind an entire agreement clause and set out the relevant case law as follows (at 614 to 615):

> 7. The purpose of an entire agreement clause is to preclude a party to a written agreement from threshing through the undergrowth and finding, in the course of negotiations, some (chance) remark or statement (often long-forgotten or difficult to recall or explain) upon which to found a claim, such as the present, to the existence of a collateral warranty. The entire agreement clause obviates the occasion for any such search and the peril to the contracting parties posed by the need that may arise in its absence to conduct such a search. For such a clause constitutes a binding agreement between the parties that the full contractual terms are to be found in the document containing the clause and not elsewhere, and that, accordingly, any promises or assurances made in the course of the negotiations (which, in the absence of such a clause, might have effect as a collateral warranty) shall have no contractual force, save in so arc as they are reflected and given effect in that document. The operation of the clause is not to render evidence of the collateral warranty inadmissible in evidence . . . it is to denude what would otherwise constitute a collateral warranty of legal effect.

3.131 In *AXA Sun Life Services plc v Campbell Martin Ltd & ors,*[59] AXA claimed damages due under several agreements, in which the defendant companies had agreed to provide specified financial services as AXA's agents. The defendant companies counterclaimed for loss and damages based on

57. This was briefly discussed in Chapter 2.
58. [2000] 2 Lloyd's Rep 611.
59. [2011] EWCA Civ 133. This English case was referred to in both *Montrio Ltd Another v Tse Ping Shun David* [2013] 4 HKC 505 and *FCL Development Pte Ltd and Another v Lai Yuen Ling and Others* [2015] HKCA 131. Unfortunately, neither of the decision turned on considering the relevant principles identified in *AXA*.

AXA's negligent misrepresentation, and/or breach of collateral warranties, and/or breach of implied terms of the agreements. AXA argued that the entire agreement clause in the agreements effectively precluded its liability because the clause would 'supersede any prior promises, agreements, representations, undertakings or implications whether made orally or in writing . . . relating to the subject matter of the agreement'.

3.132 At first instance, the court held that the clause did not preclude the defendant companies from relying on their grounds in the counterclaim.

3.133 On appeal, Rix LJ conducted a comprehensive analysis of entire agreement clauses. His Lordship cited with approval the statement of Lightman J that the purpose of entire agreement clause does not preclude a claim in misrepresentation, as the denial of contractual force to a statement cannot affect the status of the statement as a misrepresentation.[60]

3.134 Rix LJ further cited with approval the case of *BskyB Ltd v HP Enterprise Services UK Ltd*,[61] in which Ramsey J had also considered the jurisprudence on entire agreement clauses and concluded that the clause did not exclude liability for non-fraudulent misrepresentation because 'while there is a reference to representations, there is nothing in the clause that indicates it is intended to take away a right to rely on misrepresentations . . . I consider that clear words are needed to exclude a liability for negligent misrepresentation and that this clause does not include any such wording.' Rix LJ found this applicable to the *AXA* case.

3.135 The implication of the *AXA* case is that each case is only authority for the particular wording of the clause under consideration; however, it is possible to extract key themes from the decision that are applicable to all entire agreement clause cases.

3.136 First, a clear statement is required to effectively exclude liability for misrepresentation. For example, this can be done by stating that no representations were made in relation to the parties' agreement; or that there has been no reliance on representations; or by an express exclusion of liability for misrepresentations.

3.137 Second, in the absence of such statement, and particularly where the word 'representation' is embedded among other words relating to contractual obligations, the entire agreement statement will not in itself be sufficient to exclude liability for misrepresentation.

60. *Inntrepreneur Pub Co (GL) v East Crown Ltd* (supra). This is a view that appears to be shared by Hong Kong courts. See for example *Glory Gold Ltd v Star Development Ltd* [2008] 2 HKLRD 416; *Yang Dandan v Hong Kong Resort Co Ltd* [2015] 6 HKC 126.

61. [2010] EWHC 86 (TCC).

Non-reliance clause[62]

3.138 Another common technique to avoid claims in misrepresentation rests upon clauses in an agreement that seek to negative one or more elements of misrepresentation. These are typically known as non-reliance clauses.

3.139 While the wording of such clauses will vary from agreement to agreement, the material portion of such clauses invariably states that the claimant has not relied on the representation in question.

3.140 For example:

> Parties agree that neither party has placed any reliance whatsoever on any representations, agreements, statements or understandings whether oral or in writing made prior to the date of this contract other than those expressly incorporated in this contract.

3.141 The wording of the non-reliance clause must be clear in its intended effect. As Jacob J stated in in *Thomas Witter Ltd v TBP Industries Ltd*:[63]

> [I]f a clause is to have the effect of excluding or reducing remedies for damaging untrue statements then the party seeking that protection cannot be mealy-mouthed in his clause. He must bring it home that he is limiting his liability for falsehoods he may have told.

3.142 At present, it would appear a party may only exclude liability in the case of fraud or deceit if the non-reliance clause is very clearly worded and the deceit is not that of a party to the contract itself.

3.143 In *HIH Casualty and General Insurance Ltd v Chase Manhattan Bank*,[64] Lord Bingham said:

> [I]f a party to a written contract seeks to exclude the ordinary consequences of fraudulent or dishonest misrepresentations or deceit by his agent, acting as such, inducing the making of the contract, such intention must be expressed in clear and unmistakable terms on the face of the contract . . . General words, however comprehensive the legal analyst might find them to be, will not serve: the language used must be such as will alert a commercial party to the extraordinary bargain he is invited to make.

62. Presently there is limited Hong Kong jurisprudence specifically addressing non-reliance clauses and misrepresentation. In the context of financial investment, the Court of Appeal held that a bank owed its customers advisory duties in recommending investment products, despite the non-reliance or non-advisory clauses in the client agreements, because such clauses were unconscionable under the Unconscionable Contracts Ordinance (Cap 458) and unreasonable under CECO.

63. [1996] 2 ALL ER 573.

64. [2003] HKHL 6.

Misrepresentation Ordinance and Control of Exemption Clauses Ordinance

3.144 Importantly, section 4 of the Misrepresentation Ordinance limits the scope in which a party can exclude liability for misrepresentation in an agreement. It states:

> If a contract contains a term which would exclude or restrict—
>
> (a) any liability to which a party to a contract may be subject by reason of any misrepresentation made by him before the contract was made; or
>
> (b) any remedy available to another party to the contract by reason of such a misrepresentation,
>
> that term shall be of no effect except in so far as it satisfies the requirement of reasonableness as stated in section 3(1) of the Control of Exemption Clauses Ordinance (Cap 71); and it is for the person claiming that the term satisfies that requirement to show that it does.

3.145 Section 3(1) of CECO states:

> The reasonableness test
>
> (1) In relation to a contract term, the requirement of reasonableness for the purposes of this Ordinance and section 4 of the Misrepresentation Ordinance (Cap. 284) is satisfied only if the court or arbitrator determines that the term was a fair and reasonable one to be included having regard to the circumstances which were, or ought reasonably to have been, known to or in the contemplation of the parties when the contract was made.

3.146 There are several noteworthy points in relation to section 4 of the Misrepresentation Ordinance.

3.147 First, a contract term seeking to exclude or exempt liability or any remedy for misrepresentation must satisfy the same test of reasonableness as operates in the CECO.

3.148 Second, if a clause, upon its proper construction, means it only allows written terms to supersede all previous written and oral agreements and representations, then section 4 of the Misrepresentation Ordinance will not be engaged as the clause is not aimed at limiting or excluding liability.[65]

3.149 Third, reading section 4 of the Misrepresentation Ordinance in conjunction with section 3 of the Control of Exemption Clauses Ordinance requires examining the specific term of the contract and then determining whether the term was fair and reasonable upon considering the circumstances which were, or ought reasonably to have been, known to or in the contemplation of the parties when the agreement was made.

65. *Yang Dandan v Hong Kong Resort Co Ltd* [2015] 6 HKC 126 at para. 77.

3.150 In the case of *Green Park Properties Ltd v Dorku Ltd*,[66] in an attempt to deny liability, the defendant vendor company had attempted to rely on clause 12 of the provisional agreement for sale and purchase, which stated; '[t]his Agreement supersedes all prior negotiations, representation, understanding and agreements of the parties hereto.'

3.151 At first instance,[67] Cheung J observed that the director of the defendant vendor company knew that the yard was not part of the property, yet he allowed agents to show the property to the plaintiff without advising the agent in advance. Furthermore, the director should have been aware that the tenancy plan gave a misleading impression to the plaintiff purchaser yet he did nothing to dispel any misunderstanding. There was nothing that put the plaintiff purchaser on enquiry about the yard.

3.152 The judge held that clause 12 of the provisional agreement for sale and purchase failed to satisfy the reasonableness test under CECO. As a result, the plaintiff purchaser could rescind the agreement, despite the fact that the defendant vendor company's title to Portion A was not defective because the property to be conveyed did not include the yard.

3.153 On appeal,[68] it was held that the defendant vendor company had intended to sell and convey Portion A inclusive of the yard, which was a common area, to the plaintiff purchaser. As this could not ultimately be done on completion, there was a defect in the title. The Court of Final Appeal agreed with this analysis and held on that alone the plaintiff purchaser was entitled to rescind the provisional sale and purchase agreement.[69]

3.154 In *obiter*, Litton NPJ found it necessary to express his anxiety regarding Cheung J's approach to section 4 of the Misrepresentation Ordinance and section 3 of CECO:

> 27. As can be seen, what s 4 of the Misrepresentation Ordinance, combined with s 3 of the Control of Exemption Clauses Ordinance, looks to is the contract term: in this case clause 12 which says that the agreement of 14 April 1998 supersedes all prior negotiations, representations etc. The reasonableness test is satisfied if the judge concludes that the term was fair and reasonable having regard to the circumstances which were, or ought reasonably to have been, known to or in the contemplation of the parties when the agreement was made. What might those circumstances be? In this case they would include the circumstances surrounding real estate dealings in Hong Kong known to both parties bearing on whether it was fair and reasonable for a term like clause 12 to be included in a standard form of provisional agreement put forward by real estate agents for the parties' signature.

66. [2001] 1 HKLRD 139; [2000] 4 HKC 538.
67. *Green Park Properties Ltd v Dorku Ltd* [2000] 2 HKLRD 400.
68. *Green Park Properties Ltd v Dorku Ltd* [2001] 1 HKLRD 139; [2000] 4 HKC 538.
69. *Green Park Properties Ltd v Dorku Ltd* [2001] 4 HKCFAR 448.

> But this was not how the judge approached the matter. He concluded that clause 12 was of no effect because (i) [the defendant's director] knew that the yard was 'not included as part of the property'; (ii) [the defendant's director] allowed the agents to show the property to the purchasers without advising the agents of this in advance; (iii) he should have been aware that the plan was misleading; (iv) there was nothing on the ground to put the purchasers on enquiry as to the yard. These factors bear on the seriousness of [the defendant's director]'s conduct leading to the representation being made by the agents at the time of the inspection: They were not circumstances known to or in the contemplation of the parties in terms of s 3(1) of the Control of Exemption Clauses Ordinance.

3.155 While the case did not turn on Litton NPJ's *obiter* comments, it is submitted that his observations are more consistent with the language of the relevant ordinances.

4

Structure and Format of Construction Contracts

Solomon Lam

Contract Documents

4.1 Construction contracts in Hong Kong come in different forms. For smaller projects, contract documents may consist of only quotations and letters of acceptance. For larger projects or public works projects, contract documents can comprise large piles of different documents.

4.2 A typical construction contract for larger projects includes the following documents:[1]

- Articles of agreement
- Conditions of Contract
- Plans and drawings
- Specifications
- Bills of quantities or schedule of rates
- Other documents, such as correspondence, tender queries and responses, etc.

Articles of Agreement

4.3 The articles of agreement usually set out the date, the parties, the intended works, and the contract price.[2] The articles may also list the names or descriptions of architects, engineers, surveyors or contract administrators and set out their respective roles. Ideally, these will fully match the names or descriptions appearing in the other contract documents.

4.4 The articles of agreement usually contain a signature page for the parties to sign. In this regard, there are two points to note. The first is whether words such as 'signed, sealed, and delivered' appear on the signature

1. Stephen Furst and Vivian Ramsey, *Keating on Construction Contracts*, 10th ed. (Sweet & Maxwell, 2016) at paras. 1-016 to 022.
2. Stephen Furst and Vivian Ramsey, *Keating on Construction Contracts*, 10th ed. (Sweet & Maxwell, 2016) at para. 1-017.

page. If yes, it is likely that the construction contracts are a deed, which gives parties a limitation period of 12 years starting from the accrual date of a cause of action, as opposed to six years for other construction contracts.

4.5 The second point to note is the authority of the signatories. This is important when the parties dispute whether there is a valid contract formed between the parties. An example can be seen in the case of *Incorporated Owners of Hamden Court v Mega Miles Construction Company Ltd.*[3] In that case, the employer disputed that the four signatories signed on the construction contract had the authority to bind it, such that there was no valid contract and no valid arbitration agreement between the parties.

4.6 It is not very common for parties to a construction agreement to dispute that there is a valid contract between them. More commonly, parties dispute whether a person has authority to order variations or additional works on behalf of an employer.

4.7 There are basically two types of authority. One is actual authority; the other is apparent authority or ostensible authority. Actual authority concerns whether a person is authorised under law or under contract to sign a contract or order a variation.

4.8 The doctrine of apparent or ostensible authority operates to hold the principal to the acts of the agent where the principal represents to a third party that the agent has authority to act on its behalf. This applies even if the agent commits a forgery in the course of an act within its apparent authority. It is a question of fact rather than a question of law as to whether the person making a representation has authority to do so on behalf of the principal. Where this applies, the principal is unable to sue on a contract formed by the act of an agent unless such act has been ratified by the principal. The legal principles regulating representations are set out in *Chitty on Contracts—Hong Kong Specific Contracts*:[4]

1. The representation must be made by words or conduct. The representation can be express or it may be implied from surrounding circumstances.
2. The representation must be one of fact and not of law.
3. The representation must have been made by the principal or a person who had actual authority to act on behalf of him. On its own, a representation by the agent himself shall not suffice to bind the principal.
4. The representation be made to a third party.

3. [2015] 5 HKC 179.
4. 3rd ed., at para. 1-050.

5. The third party must be induced by the representation to enter into the contract. The principal will not be liable if the third party chose not to investigate the agent's authority if the opportunity arose, or was put on notice by the specifics of the transaction, or in fact knew that the agent was acting outside the boundaries of its powers.

4.9 In *Freeman and Lockyer v Buckhurst Park Properties (Mangnal) Ltd*,[5] Diplock LJ explained in detail the law of actual and apparent authorities, commenting on the representation creating apparent authority:

> The representation which created 'apparent' authority may take a variety of forms of which the commonest is representation by conduct, that is, by permitting the agent to act in some way in the conduct of the principal's business with other persons. By so doing the principal represents to anyone who becomes aware that the agent is so acting that the agent has authority to enter on behalf of the principal into contracts with other persons of the kind which an agent so acting in the conduct of his principal's business has usually actual authority to enter into.

4.10 He continued:

> The commonest form of representation by a principal creating an 'apparent' authority of an agent is by conduct, namely, by permitting the agent to act in the management or conduct of the principal's business. Thus, if in the case of a company the board of directors who have 'actual' authority under the memorandum and articles of association to manage the company's business permit the agent to act in the management or conduct of the company's business, they thereby represent to all persons dealing with such agent that he has authority to enter on behalf of the corporation into contracts of a kind which an agent authorised to do acts of the kind which he is in fact permitted to do usually enters into in the ordinary course of such business.

4.11 In *Thanakharn Kasikorn Thai Chamkat (Mahachon) v Akai Holdings Ltd (No 2)*,[6] the Court of Final Appeal held that there were three issues to resolve in determining whether the executive chairman and CEO Mr Ting had apparent authority to commit his company Akai to the Switch Transaction:

> 47. Probably the main point of principle which divides the parties centres on what state of mind is required in order to establish that the Bank 'justifiably relied' on Mr Ting's authority. Another issue of principle is the extent, if any, to which a third party who claims to have dealt with an alleged apparent agent can rely on unauthorised statements made by the agent as to his authority to justify the contention that he had authority to commit the principal. The third issue of principle concerns the evidence required from the Bank to show that it relied on the apparent authority of Mr Ting.

5. [1964] 2 QB 480 at pp. 502–506.
6. (2010) 13 HKCFAR 479.

4.12 As to the first issue, the test was one of 'irrationality'. Lord Neuberger of Abbotsbury NPJ said:

> 52. In a commercial context, absent dishonesty or irrationality, a person should be entitled to rely on what he is told: this may occasionally produce harsh results, but it enables people engaged in business to know where they stand.

4.13 He concluded:

> 62. I conclude that it is open to the Bank to rely on Mr Ting's apparent authority (if he had such authority) unless the Bank's belief in that connection was dishonest or irrational (which includes turning a blind eye and being reckless).

4.14 As to the second issue, Lord Neuberger NPJ said:

> 68. The effect of those decisions appears to be that, at least in the Courts of England and Wales, it is very unlikely that a third party could establish apparent authority on the part of an alleged agent by relying on the agent's own unauthorised statement to clothe the agent with authority. The judgment of Goff LJ and the speech of Lord Keith of Kinkel in *Armagas* [1986] AC 717, 730H–732F and 777C–778D indicate great scepticism as to the notion that an agent could clothe himself with authority in this way. Having said at [1986] AC 717, 777D that there might be 'very rare and unusual' circumstances in which this might happen.

4.15 As to the third issue, Lord Neuberger NPJ said:

> 75. In my view, once a third party has established that the alleged agent had apparent authority, i.e. that the principal held out the alleged agent as having authority to bind the principal, and that the third party has entered into a contract with the alleged agent on behalf of the principal, then, in the absence of any evidence or indication to the contrary, it would be an unusual case where reliance was not presumed.

4.16 Given the above, it is necessary to consider and state clearly who would be authorised under a construction contract, and the scope and extent of authorities conferred, in order to avoid disputes in the future.

Conditions of Contract

4.17 Traditionally, the word 'condition' bears legal meaning under contract law. A 'condition' is a more important term of a contract, a breach of which will result in the termination of a contract. This is in contrast with a 'warranty', a less important contract term.

4.18 In the context of construction contracts, one would not expect that a breach of a condition of contract will necessarily render the contract terminated. Therefore, the conditions of contract may be seen merely as part of the ordinary contract terms. Still, conditions serve as an important skeleton to construction contracts, as they usually contain most of the essential terms set out in a framework.

4.19 Conditions of contract may be incorporated into a construction contract by reference to a standard form of general conditions of contract. Apart from general conditions of contract which normally adopt standard forms, a construction contract usually includes special conditions of contract written specifically for a particular construction project, which add to or amend the general conditions of contract. There may also be boilerplate clauses for individual employers or consultants.

Standard Forms of Conditions of Contract

4.20 The use of standard form contracts is very common in building and engineering projects in Hong Kong, especially for the general conditions of contract. The use of standard forms enables both parties to adopt familiar clauses with known implications as they have received judicial interpretation.[7]

4.21 However, the use of standard forms has been criticised by the English courts. For example, in *Amalgamated Building Contractors Ltd v Waltham Holy Cross UDC*,[8] Lord Denning criticised the RIBA form as giving rise to interpretation problems as it left the court unable to ascertain the intentions of the parties. Another example of criticism can be found in *Peak Construction (Liverpool) Ltd v McKinney Foundations Ltd*.[9]

4.22 For works funded by and public authorities of the Hong Kong government, the standard forms of construction contracts commonly adopted are the General Conditions of Contract for Civil Engineering Works (1999) and the General Conditions of Contract for Building Works (1999). Clause 86 of both standard forms is an arbitration clause.

4.23 The New Engineering Contract (NEC) has also been in use by the Hong Kong government since 2009. The government has published a practice note in relation to the use of the NEC standard form for public works project and published Standard Amendments to NEC ECC Standard Document and Additional Conditions of Contract.

4.24 For privately funded construction projects in Hong Kong, the most commonly adopted standard forms are the Agreement and Schedule of Conditions of Building Contract (Standard Form of Building Contract) for

7. Brian Gilchrist, *Chitty on Contracts Hong Kong Specific Contracts*, 5th ed. (Sweet & Maxwell, 2016) at para. 8-017.
8. [1952] 2 All ER 452.
9. (1970) 1 BLR 111.

Use in Hong Kong, Private Edition.[10] This set has 1986, 1999, 2005, and 2006 editions. The 1986 edition followed the UK Joint Contracts Tribunal 1963 standard form of contract.[11] The 1999 edition was drafted by the Hong Kong Institute of Surveyors with the Hong Kong Institute of Architects in substitution for the Royal Institution of Chartered Surveyors.[12] The 2005 edition was an updated version designed for contracts 'with' quantities, whereas the 2006 edition was an updated version design for contracts 'without' quantities.

4.25 There are also standard forms of subcontracts. These are the Subcontract for Building Works (2000 edition) published by the Hong Kong government for public works and the Standard Form of Domestic Subcontract (2008 edition) published by the Hong Kong Construction Association for private projects.

4.26 Certain terms are usually contained in the standard forms of conditions of contract. Parties will want to give special consideration to certain clauses at the drafting and negotiation stages, including on liquidated damages term and dispute resolution.

4.27 An important certificate to note is the certificate of non-completion to be issued by the architect under clause 24 in the 2005 edition with quantities and the 2006 edition without quantities of the Agreement and Schedule of Conditions of Building Contract (Standard Form of Building Contract) for Use in Hong Kong, which is the condition precedent of imposing liquidated damages on the contractor. There is no such a requirement under clause 52 of the General Conditions of Contract for Civil Engineering Works (1999) and the General Conditions of Contract for Building Works (1999).

4.28 When a dispute or difference arises between the parties, it is very important to first look at the dispute resolution clause to see if there is an arbitration agreement. If there is, the parties should go to arbitration to resolve their dispute instead of going to court.

4.29 If there is an arbitration agreement, it is also prudent to find out whether there is any condition precedent such as mediation or completion of the works before a party may commence an arbitration against the other party.

4.30 It is said that Schedule 2 of the Arbitration Ordinance (Cap 609) does not apply when the arbitration agreement does not expressly state that the parties opt in to Schedule 2 or state that the arbitration will be a domestic

---

10. Gary Soo, *Construction Law and Practice in Hong Kong*, 4th ed. (Sweet & Maxwell, 2018) at para. 19.013.
11. Geoffrey Ma, *Arbitration in Hong Kong: A Practical Guide*, 4th ed. (Sweet & Maxwell, 2017) at para. 21.031.
12. Geoffrey Ma, *Arbitration in Hong Kong: A Practical Guide*, 4th ed. (Sweet & Maxwell, 2017) at para. 21.034.

arbitration.[13] It is thus prudent to make the application of those provisions express if the parties wish to adopt them.

4.31 There is an appeal procedure under section 5(1) of Schedule 2 of the Arbitration Ordinance (Cap 609) for appealing on a point of law.[14] Without adopting Schedule 2 expressly, the general position is that the losing party is required to challenge an arbitral award under section 81(2) of the Arbitration Ordinance (Cap 609) incorporating Article 34 of the UNCITRAL Model Law. As compared to appeal under section 5 of Schedule 2 of the Arbitration Ordinance, section 81 of the Arbitration Ordinance does not allow appeal on point of law or fact even if the arbitrator was wrong.

4.32 Standard forms of general conditions of contract normally contain dispute resolution clauses, and the dispute resolution clauses contained in standard forms commonly used in Hong Kong are discussed below as illustrations.

4.33 At the drafting and negotiation stages, if the parties consider the dispute resolution clauses contained in the standard form do not reflect their intention and agreement, they should replace or adjust the clauses by special conditions of contract or in other contract documents.

4.34 The dispute resolution clause contained in the 2005 edition with quantities and 2006 edition without quantities of the Agreement and Schedule of Conditions of Building Contract (Standard Form of Building Contract) for Use in Hong Kong is clause 41.

4.35 Clause 41.4 is the arbitration clause which expressly states that the arbitration shall be a domestic arbitration. Therefore, Schedule 2 of the Arbitration Ordinance (Cap 609) will apply.

4.36 Before a party can commence an arbitration, it is required to refer the dispute to the designated representatives (clause 41.2) and mediation (clause 41.3). Clause 41.5 also sets out certain timing requirements in commencing the arbitration.

4.37 The dispute resolution clause in the General Conditions of Contract for Civil Engineering Works (1999) and General Conditions of Contract for Building Works (1999) is clause 86. Clause 86(2) is the arbitration clause.[15] Clause 86(6) also provides that the arbitration will be a domestic

13. Geoffrey Ma, *Arbitration in Hong Kong: A Practical Guide*, 4th ed. (Sweet & Maxwell, 2017) at paras. 21.035–21.036.
14. Section 5(1) of Schedule 2 of the Arbitration Ordinance (Cap 609) states that '[s]ubject to section 6 of this Schedule, a party to arbitral proceedings may appeal to the Court on a question of law arising out of an award made in the arbitral proceedings.'
15. Clause 86(2) states: '(2) If the matter cannot be resolved by mediation, or if either the employer or the Contractor do not wish the matter to be referred to mediation then either the employer or the Contractor may within the time specified herein require that the matter

arbitration, therefore, Schedule 2 of the Arbitration Ordinance (Cap 609) will apply.[16]

4.38 Clause 86(1)[17] provides that, before commencing an arbitration, the parties need to refer their dispute to the engineer for determination. It also mentions mediation; however, its wording does not suggest that going to mediation is a condition precedent before one can commence an arbitration.

4.39 The NEC standard forms are different. The dispute resolution clause for contracts outside the UK in NEC3 Engineering and Construction Contract is W1 clause. It provides for dispute resolution by way of adjudication first and then by a tribunal to be agreed by the parties in the contract data. If the parties agreed in the contract data that the tribunal shall be an arbitral tribunal, then it will become an arbitration clause.

---

shall be referred to arbitration in accordance with and subject to the provisions of the Arbitration Ordinance (Cap. 341) or any statutory modification thereof for the time being in force and any such reference shall be deemed to be a submission to arbitration within the meaning of such Ordinance. Any reference to arbitration shall be made within 90 days of: (a) the receipt of a request for mediation and subsequently the recipient of such request having failed to respond, or (b) the refusal to mediate, or (c) the failure of the mediation proceedings to produce a settlement acceptable to the employer and the contractor, or (d) the abandonment of the mediation, or (e) the engineer failing to make a decision for a period of 90 days after being so requested to do so and subsequently neither the employer nor the Contractor having requested mediation, or (f) the receipt of a notice of a decision by the engineer and subsequently neither the employer nor the Contractor having requested mediation.'

16. Clause 86(6) states that: 'The reference to arbitration under sub-clause (2) of this Clause shall be a domestic arbitration for the purposes of Part II of the Arbitration Ordinance (Cap. 341).'
17. Clause 86(1) states that: 'If any dispute or difference of any kind whatsoever shall arise between the employer and the contractor in connection with or arising out of the contract or the carrying out of the Works including any dispute as to any decision, instruction, order, direction, certificate or valuation by the engineer whether during the progress of the Works or after their completion and whether before or after the termination, abandonment or breach of the Contract, it shall be referred to and settled by the engineer who shall state his decision in writing and give notice of the same to the employer and the Contractor. Unless the contract shall have been already terminated or abandoned the contractor shall in every case continue to proceed with the Works with all due diligence and he shall give effect forthwith to every such decision of the engineer unless and until the same shall be revised in mediation or arbitration as hereinafter provided. Such decision shall be final and binding upon the contractor and the employer unless either of them shall require that the matter be referred to mediation or arbitration as hereinafter provided. If the engineer shall fail to give such decision for a period of 28 days after being requested to do so or if either the employer or the contractor be dissatisfied with any such decision of the engineer then either the employer or the contractor may within 28 days after receiving notice of such decision, or within 28 days after the expiry of the said decision period of 28 days, as the case may be, request that the matter be referred to mediation in accordance with and subject to The Government of the Hong Kong Special Administrative Region Construction Mediation Rules (the Mediation Rules) or any modification thereof being in force at the date of such request.'

4.40 Clause 32.9 in the 2005 edition with quantities and the 2006 edition without quantities of the Agreement and Schedule of Conditions of Building Contract (Standard Form of Building Contract) for Use in Hong Kong provides that the Final Certificate shall be conclusive evidence on materials, goods, workmanship, and final account. However, clause 41.6 expressly provides that the arbitrator can review and revise certificate of the architect.

4.41 Clause 80 of the General Conditions of Contract for Civil Engineering Works (1999)[18] and the General Conditions of Contract for Building Works (1999), on the other hand, expressly states that the Maintenance Certificate cannot be seen as relieving the contractor's liability.

4.42 There is similar wording giving an arbitrator power to review certificates issued by the engineer in clause 86(3)[19] of the General Conditions of Contract for Civil Engineering Works (1999) and the General Conditions of Contract for Building Works (1999).

Plans and Drawings

4.43 The extent of the details contained in plans and drawings depends on whether the employer engages an architect or engineer before tendering out the works to contractors. Plans and drawings in some contracts may show the works in full detail,[20] whereas in other contracts there may be only a few schematic plans and drawings.

4.44 Plans and drawings are usually prepared by architects and engineers. They may specify certain specifications of works on the 'notes' as part of the plans and drawings. Uncommonly, there may be inconsistencies between these notes and other specifications.

---

18. Clause 80(3) states that '(3) [t]he issue of any certificate including the maintenance certificate shall not be taken as relieving either the Contractor or the employer from any liability the one towards the other arising out of or in any way connected with the performance of their respective obligations under the Contract. Provided that the employer shall not be liable to the Contractor for any matter or thing arising out of or in connection with the Contract or the execution of the Works unless the Contractor shall have made a claim in relation thereto in accordance with the time limits specified in Clause 50 or Clause 64.'
19. Clause 86(3) states that '[t]he arbitrator appointed shall have full power to open up, review and revise any decision (other than a decision under Clause 46(3) not to vary the Works), instruction, order, direction, certificate or valuation by the engineer and neither party shall be limited in the proceedings before such arbitrator to the evidence or arguments put before the engineer for the purpose of obtaining his decision above referred to. Save as provided for in sub-clause (4) of this Clause no steps shall be taken in the reference to the arbitrator until after the completion or alleged completion of the Works unless with the written consent of the employer and the Contractor.'
20. Stephen Furst and Sir Vivian Ramsey, *Keating on Construction Contracts*, 10th ed. (Sweet & Maxwell, 2016) at para. 1-018.

4.45 Another problematic area is the issuance of construction drawings, working drawings or drawing amendments which are different from tender drawings in the construction period. It is said that whether such drawings amount to a variation or delay and disruption is a difficult question of fact.[21]

Specifications

4.46 Specifications refer to a document which describes the work to be done and the goods to be supplied.[22] Specifications contain technical requirements on the testing and performance of materials, the methodology for carrying out the works, and the completed works.

4.47 Many construction contracts in Hong Kong adopt standard form general specifications together with particular specifications written specifically for individual projects.

4.48 Commonly used general specifications in Hong Kong include the General Specification for Civil Engineering Works (2006 edition) published by the Civil Engineering and Development Department of the Hong Kong government, General Specification for Building (2003, 2007, 2012 or 2017 editions) published by the Architectural Services Department of the Hong Kong government, and other general specifications published by the Architectural Services Department of the Hong Kong government.

4.49 Another form of specification comes in the form of employer's requirements in design and build contracts. Employer's requirements provide objectives to be achieved rather than the method or design required to attain the objective. Employer's requirements must be clear and concise, but if they are too prescriptive they may dilute or negate the contractor's design obligations or restrict the contractor's choice of solutions.[23]

Bills of Quantities or Schedule of Rates

4.50 Bills of quantities quantify the works in detail and are ordinarily prepared in accordance with an agreed standard method of measurement. Their purpose is to put into words every obligation or service which will be required in carrying out the building project. They may form part of the contract; express words in the articles of agreement or conditions of contract are required to make the bills of quantities a contract document.

21. Nicholas Dennys and Robert Clay, *Hudson's Building and Engineering Contracts*, 13th ed. (Sweet & Maxwell 2018) at para. 3-014.
22. Stephen Furst and Sir Vivian Ramsey, *Keating on Construction Contracts*, 10th ed. (Sweet & Maxwell, 2016) at para. 1-019.
23. Nicholas Dennys and Robert Clay, *Hudson's Building and Engineering Contracts*, 13th ed. (Sweet & Maxwell, 2018) at para. 3-019.

They often contain a preamble which describes the methods of measurement of the works adopted in their preparation or the basis on which they are to be priced.[24]

4.51 The commonly used standard methods of measurement are the Standard Method of Measurement for Building Elements published by the Architectural Services Department of the Hong Kong government, the Standard Method of Measurement for Civil Engineering Works published by the Civil Engineering and Development Department of the Hong Kong government, and the Hong Kong Standard Method of Measurement of Building Works published by the Hong Kong Institute of Surveyors.

4.52 As always, contractors must be careful in filling in the price and rates on bills of quantities. In *Henry Boot Construction Ltd v Alstom Combined Cycles Ltd* [2000] CLC 1147, it was held that the rates and price stated in the bills of quantities were not subject to rectification by reason of mistake.

4.53 However, when construction contracts provide a mechanism for revising the rates in the bills of quantities ('re-rating'), the court can look at how the rate was built up in those rates stated in the bills of quantities.[25]

4.54 The methods of measurement are important in the sense that they define the item coverage of a priced item under the bills of quantities.

4.55 Ambiguities in the item coverage in construction contracts give rise to disputes between contracting parties.

4.56 The applicability of an item in the bills of quantities to a particular piece of the works is another problematic area in practice which may cause disputes between the parties in the valuation of work done. An example can be seen in the recent Court of Appeal case of *Chun Wo Construction & Engineering Co Ltd v The Hong Kong Housing Authority*.[26]

4.57 In that case, the contractor plaintiffs were required to carry out maintenance, improvement and refurbishment works in public housing estates for the defendant. From time to time, work orders would be issued by the defendant instructing the plaintiffs to carry out specific tasks. The case was concerned with work orders issued for the replacement of sliding window hinges used to affix aluminium window sashes to the window frames of flats in housing estates. The contracts between the parties contained a schedule of rates. Though the parties agreed that works had been done and work orders should be valued pursuant to the schedule of rates, they disagreed on which specific rates in the schedule of rates should be used

24. Stephen Furst and Sir Vivian Ramsey, *Keating on Construction Contracts*, 10th ed. (Sweet & Maxwell, 2016) at para. 1-020.
25. *Maeda Corp v Government of the HKSAR* [2014] 1 HKLRD 1.
26. [2019] HKCA 369.

in valuing the works. The parties ended up in arbitration and appeals to the High Court and Court of Appeal.

4.58 Therefore, on top of standard methods of measurement, parties should specifically draft the bills of quantities together with a document explaining the item coverage of every item appeared in the bills of quantities and how to apply the rates stated in the bills of quantities.

4.59 The bills of quantities consist of different columns, namely description, quantities, unit, rate and price. Normally, the employer or its consultants prepare the bills of quantities and the tenderers fill in the prices against each item.

4.60 Some contracts are paid based on a lump sum, which is not subject to remeasurement. These contracts may incorporate a schedule of rates which will be used for valuation of additional works.[27]

4.61 In relation to the descriptions in the bills of quantities, it was held in *Hung Wan Construction Co Ltd v Hong Kong Hosing Authority*[28] that, when a contractor priced its tender based on drawings and specifications on a lump sum basis, unless there were subsequent variations, the quantity stated in the description column in the bills of quantities was irrelevant in determining the money the contractor was entitled to.

4.62 In the recent Hong Kong Court of Appeal case of *Maeda Kensetsu Kogyo Kabushiki Kaisha also known as Maeda Corporation & Another v Bauer Hong Kong Ltd*,[29] there was a dispute between the main contractor and the subcontractor in relation to measurement rules for diaphragm walls under the subcontract. The court noted that the contract documents were poorly drafted. The court took the practical and commercial implications into account in interpretating the contract. This case illustrates that clear drafting of measurement rules is crucial to avoiding disputes.

Missing Items

4.63 Also relating to bills of quantities or schedule of rates, a common form of dispute is the claim of missing items by contractors.

4.64 Broadly speaking, a missing or omitted item refers to the omission of an appropriate (and required) item in the bills of quantities for works or services shown or provided in the contract drawings or specifications.

4.65 This may be illustrated using the context of the General Conditions of Contract for Civil Engineering Works (1999) and the Standard Method

---

27. Stephen Furst and Sir Vivian Ramsey, *Keating on Construction Contracts*, 10th ed. (Sweet & Maxwell, 2016) at para. 1-021.
28. [2010] HKCFI 650.
29. [2020] 1 HKC 470.

of Measurement for Civil Engineering Works published by the Civil Engineering and Development Department of the Hong Kong government (the SMM). It is commonly understood that, as laid down in the General Conditions of Contract, in particular clause 59[30] and clause 61 thereof, for a missing/omitted item:

(a) the contractor is required to carry out the works of the missing/omitted item;

(b) the engineer shall correct any such omission, and ascertain and certify the value of the works actually carried out;

(c) if there is a similar item(s) in the Bills of Quantities, the missing/omitted item should be valued at the rate of such similar item(s); and

(d) if there are no similar items in the Bills of Quantities, the missing/omitted item should be valued at a rate based on the rates in the Contract so far as may be reasonable and failing which, at a rate agreed between the engineer and the contractor; and fixed by the engineer in the event that the engineer and the contractor fail to reach an agreement on a rate.

4.66 Missing or omitted item claims are quite unique to Hong Kong, since the item-coverage approach is adopted in the usual practice under the standard methods of measurement in construction contracts in Hong Kong. This type of claim is recognised in documents such as the Project Administration Handbook for Civil Engineering Works of the Works Branch of the Development Bureau.[31]

4.67 In this regard, there is the commonly known 'inclusive price principle' that has been discussed extensively in the classic practitioners' text of *Hudson's Building and Engineering Contracts* (11th ed.).

4.68 *Hudson's*,[32] noting that the description of works to be carried out is usually found in technical documents such as drawings, specifications, bills of quantities/schedule of rates, states that the definition of works to be carried out may be problematic:

> [T]he contract may omit to mention specifically work which nevertheless will inevitably and invariably be necessary in order to carry out

30. Clause 59(3) provides: 'Any error in description in the Bills of Quantities or item omitted therefrom shall not vitiate the Contract nor release the Contractor from the execution of the whole or any part of the Works according to the Drawings and Specification or from any of his obligations or liabilities under the Contract. The engineer shall correct any such error or omission, shall ascertain the value of the work actually carried out in accordance with Clause 61, and shall certify in accordance with Clause 79.'
31. See, for example, para. 7.2 of Chapter 5 of the Project Administration Handbook for Civil Engineering Works of the Works Branch of the Development Bureau (2014 ed.).
32. Ian Duncan Wallace, *Hudson's Building and Engineering Contracts*, 11th ed. (Sweet & Maxwell, 1994) at para. 4.037.

> the described work properly. In the smaller ancillary work processes this factor, given practical documentary limitations, will be present in a greater or lesser degree in virtually every construction contract. But more important items of such indispensable work may also, perhaps but not necessarily inadvertently, be omitted which more general descriptions elsewhere in the documentation may nevertheless indicate must have been included in the contract intention.

4.69 In continues:[33]

> It is proposed to consider those cases where whole items of work not shown in the technical documents maybe necessary either:
>
> (a) by implication or as a matter of interpretation of the contract as a whole in order that the final work should comply with the express requirements or descriptions in the contract documents (i.e., indispensably necessary works); or
>
> (b) to achieve completion of the described work in the face of practical difficulties or eventualities or of damage to the works during construction, or for other technical reasons (i.e., contingently necessary works).

4.70 Nevertheless, as stated, both those indispensably necessary works and contingently necessary works should, in the absence of express contrary provisions, be regarded as having been included in the contractor's pricing of the bills of quantities or schedules of rates. This principle is known as the 'inclusive price principle'.

4.71 In the same vein, it is also noteworthy that the classic text *Construction Contracts: Principles and Policies in Tort and Contract*[34] states:

> [For] example, the quantities of concrete (which from an examination of the drawings or the specification or Bills themselves, is required to be fair-faced) are set out in the Bills without any separate items for form-work or shuttering, the contractor will claim additional payment on the ground that there has been an 'omission of an item' from the Bills . . . The legal basis of this type of 'Standard Method' claim rests upon one unsatisfactory case many years ago in England where the point was in fact conceded. Even though the view has been expressed that these claims are without foundation, quantity surveyors and architects in England regularly advise their employers that such claims should be allowed . . . It should be appreciated that this type of claim only needs to be advanced where there is, by definition, no variation—in order words, where the contract as a whole indicates clearly that the particular process or expenditure is part of the described work which the contractor has to carry out. Such claims are essentially without merit, because either (a) the contractor has noticed the 'error' in the Bills when pricing, and if he intended to claim was stealing a march

33. Ibid, para. 4.038.
34. I.N. Duncan Wallace, *Construction Contracts: Principles and Policies in Tort and Contract* (Sweet & Maxwell, 1996), Vol. 1, at para. 26-11.

on both the employer and his competitors in tendering an apparently lower price, or (b) he has not noticed the 'error,' in which case his prices will in any event have included for the process or contingent expenditure involved [i.e., the inclusive price principle].

4.72 Thus, if applying the 'inclusive price principle', one view may be that a claim for a missing or omitted item of a contractor will generally fail unless there exists express provision under the contract showing the contrary.

4.73 It is noted that the applicability of this 'inclusive price principle' in an individual case (and if so the extent of its effect) has to be reviewed on a case-by-case basis, taking into account of the full circumstances of the contract, the item in issue and its surrounding circumstances.

4.74 For usual government works construction contracts, para. 1 of the general preambles at part IV of the SMM (as amended) states that the bills of quantities have been prepared in accordance with the procedure set forth in the SMM. Also, by particular preambles to the bills of quantities, corrigenda to the SMM up to, for example, the Corrigendum No 1/2007 are not uncommonly incorporated.

4.75 For those construction contracts incorporating the original (unamended) form of the SMM, such omitted item claims are readily assessed or accepted in appropriate circumstances by construction professionals in Hong Kong, notwithstanding the deemed inclusive price as expressed or attempted to have expressed in its wording. For easy reference and comparison, the wording of para. 2 of the general preambles in that original (unamended) SMM provides:

> The sub-headings and item descriptions used in the Bills of Quantities identify the work covered by the respective items, but the exact nature and extent of the work to be performed is to be ascertained by reference to the Drawings, Specification and Conditions of Contract, as the case may be, in conjunction with the matters listed against the relevant marginal headings 'Item coverage' in Part V. The rates to be inserted in the Bills of Quantities shall be deemed to be the full inclusive value for the work covered by these specific items and as covering all labour, materials, temporary work, plant, overhead charges and profit as well as the general liabilities, obligations and risks arising out of the Contract.

4.76 To enhance certainty on the matter, the SMM has been updated. With the introduction of Corrigendum No 1/2007, the general preambles to the bills of quantifies in part IV of the SMM (as amended) provides that:

> 2. Items shown in the bills of the Bills of Quantities are items of work. In these Bills of Quantities and the Method of Measurement, the headings, sub-headings, item descriptions and the matters listed against the relevant marginal headings "Item coverage" in Part V of the Method of Measurement and the Particular Preambles identify the

work covered by the respective items, but such descriptions or identifications may not be exhaustive. The exact nature and extent of an item of work must be ascertained by reference to the Drawings, Specification and Conditions of Contract, as not all requirements may be stated in the item description or its item coverage. Furthermore, whilst the item description and item coverage may make specific reference to certain Drawings and/or Specification, the item of work described is deemed to include for all requirements shown on all Drawings and/or Specification pertaining to that item of work irrespective of whether or not the Drawing and/or Specification is stated in the item description or item coverage. The item description of an item of work shall be deemed to include an item coverage for the carrying out of all work and services necessary or desirable for the satisfactory completion of such item of work in accordance with the Contract.

The rate inserted against an item of work in the bills within the Bills of Quantities shall be deemed to be the full inclusive value of executing, completing, maintaining and/or supplying such item of work including any incidental work thereto, unless expressly stated otherwise elsewhere in the Bills of Quantities. The expression "incidental work" includes, but is not limited to, the carrying out of all work and services and complying with all obligations which are specified or reasonably implied in the Contract and which are related to, arise out of or are connected with the item of work as described in its headings, sub-headings, item description and item coverage. The rates inserted against the items of work in the bills within the Bills of Quantities shall include, but are not limited to, the following:

(i) provision of labour and costs in connection therewith;

(ii) provision of plant and costs in connection therewith;

(iii) the supply, transportation, handling and storage of materials and goods;

(iv) multiple handling of any kind;

(v) sampling and testing and costs in connection therewith;

(vi) assembling, fixing, erecting, installing or placing of materials and goods in position;

(vii) preparation of surfaces and other preparatory work for follow-on activities;

(viii) wastage, bulking, shrinkage and the disposal of surplus material;

(ix) temporary protection and its subsequent removal;

(x) temporary works, including design;

(xi) taking precautions and measures as far as is reasonable and practical to prevent interference with or damage to existing structures and utilities, roads, footpaths and paved areas, watercourses and drainage systems, public and private vehicular and pedestrian accesses, trees, graves and burial urns, including the provision of alternative access, if necessary;

(xii) keeping the Works where necessary, and as near as may be practical, free of water and protected from damage due to water and from weather conditions which may adversely affect the Works, and taking measures to prevent flotation of new or existing structures;

(xiii) taking all measures required to execute the work as affected by non-tidal *open water or tidal water;*

(xiv) provision of working space and upholding the sides of excavations;

(xv) carrying out trial mixes, trial runs and all other trials, demonstrations and mock-ups;

(xvi) completion of formation and earthwork final surfaces;

(xvii) recording, taking readings, measurements and observations, and submitting to the Engineer all drawings, details of procedures and methods of construction to be used, technical literature, test certificates and any other documents or information required to be submitted under the Contract;

(xviii) in the case of materials supplied by the Employer, return of the surplus;

(xix) in the case of plant and equipment supplied by the Employer, protection, maintenance and repair of such plant and equipment while it is on the Site, costs in connection with operating such plant and equipment, and return of plant and equipment to the Employer or replacement of such plant and equipment if it is damaged beyond repair or lost;

(xx) notifying, making arrangements and liaising with all relevant government departments, authorities or other interested parties to obtain and maintain all licences and permits necessary for the execution of the Works, and costs in connection therewith including the costs of complying with the terms and conditions of the licences and permits;

(xxi) liabilities, obligations and risks involved in the execution of the Works set forth or reasonably implied in the Contract;

(xxii) establishment charges, overheads and profit;

(xxiii) testing including all expenses for site acceptance tests, factory acceptance tests and the associated cost for Engineer's inspection of the tests, tests of individual system of the Works, and completion tests of the Works;

(xxiv) commissioning;

(xxv) all cost and charge due to construction issues and constraints stated in or implied from the Contract.

4.77 From this paragraph, the traditional concept of item coverage (though still remaining) has been widely extended and the following may be noted:

(a) items of work for this purpose are those items shown in the bills of the bills of quantities;

(b) the works covered by the respective items are identified in the bills of quantities and the method of measurement, the headings, the sub-headings, item descriptions and the matters listed under the heading of 'Item Coverage' of the method of measurement and the particular preamble, though such descriptions or identifications may not be exhaustive;

(c) not all requirements may be stated in the item description or its item coverage and the exact nature and extent of an item of work must be ascertained by reference to the drawings, specifications and conditions of contract;

(d) while specific reference to drawings or specifications may or may not be made in the item description and item coverage, the item of work so described is taken to be inclusive for all requirements shown on all drawings and specifications pertaining to that item of work, including all works which are incidental in nature;

(e) incidental works are defined to include the carrying out of all work and services and complying with all obligations specified or reasonably implied in the contract and being related to, arising out of or connected with the item of work in issue;

(f) the rate inserted against an item of work shall be deemed to be the full inclusive value of executing, completing, maintaining and/or supplying such item of work including any incidental works for that item, unless expressly stated otherwise elsewhere in the bills of quantities.

4.78 The general preambles to the bills of quantities also contain the following clauses as regards measurement and item coverage:

(a) on general principles,

i. para. 3 in part II thereof provides:

Each item description used in the Bills of Quantities is to be consistent with and be compounded from one or more of the descriptive features listed in the itemisation groups in the various sections of Part V, as many of these groups or features being used as may be necessary to identity the work required, but not more than one feature from any one group may be represented in any one item description;

ii. para. 4 in part II thereof provides:

Unless expressly stated otherwise in the Contract, the Bills of Quantities are to contain all those items compounded in accordance with the foregoing paragraph 3 required to comprise the Works (apart from Provisional Sums and Prime Cost Items which may be required);

(b) on quantities, para. 3 in part III thereof provides: 'The quantities shall be computed net from the Drawings, unless otherwise stated in the Contract, and no allowance shall be made for bulking, shrinkage or waste';

(c) on amendments to the method of measurement, para. 10 in part III thereof provides: 'Any methods of measurement which are not in accordance with or included in the Method of Measurement shall be stated in a Particular Preamble to the Bills of Quantities';

(d) on method of measurement, para. 1 in part IV thereof provides: 'These Bills of Quantities have been prepared in accordance with the procedures set forth in the Standard Method of Measurement for Civil Engineer Works, 1992 Edition (the Government of the Hong Kong Special Administrative Region), hereafter referred to as the "Method of Measurement"';

(e) on measurement, para. 3 in part IV thereof provides: 'The measurement of work shall be computed net from the Drawings unless stated otherwise in the Method of Measurement';

(f) on item coverage, para. 4 in part IV thereof provides: 'If any item coverage includes reference to work which is the subject of item coverages elsewhere in the Method of Measurement, then the combined item coverages shall apply'.

4.79 From the above, it is obvious that it is much more difficult to claim for missing or omitted items. Yet, one may ask what types of omitted item claims, if any, may still be validly pursued? Applying the governing principles for interpretation of contracts, the following may be observed in relation to missing/omitted item claims in the context of the SMM (as amended).

(a) The contract, including the SMM (as amended) and the bills of quantities, shall be read as a whole and as a one-piece consistent document.

(b) As regards the all-inclusive price principle,

i. para. 2 in the general preambles at part IV of the SMM (as amended) does provide that its operation is subject to the wording 'unless expressly stated otherwise elsewhere in the Bills of Quantities';

ii. para. 1 in the general preambles at part IV of the SMM (as amended) does make it clear that '[t]hese Bills of Quantities have been prepared in accordance with the procedures set forth in [the SMM (as amended)]';

iii. para. 3 in the general preambles at part IV of the SMM (as amended) is of similar effect, as reinforced by para. 10 thereof; and

iv. in various sections of the SMM (as amended), separate items are expressly stated to be required to be provided for individual items of the works under the heading 'Itemisation' and, for such separate items, the item coverage is indeed listed out.

(c) Therefore, as a general principle, for an item of works to be carried out (whether shown in drawings, specifications or elsewhere in the contract) that should have been separately itemised as required by the SMM (as amended) but is missing/not found in the bills of the bills of quantities can become an 'error in description in the Bills of Quantities or item omitted' under clause 59(3) of the Conditions of Contract.

(d) Also, with a detailed list of item coverage included in all items, subject to circumstances of individual situations, there can be cases where the aforesaid principles of *expressio unius est exclusio alterius* become operative and/or *ejusdem generis*, particularly when the descriptions or listing for the item coverage of the same class or nature of works item in the bills of quantities are not clear enough, may become operative to allow items of works (not otherwise falling within the definition of incidental works) of the same category of nature but not expressly mentioned and/or of a sufficiently different nature to those listed in the item coverage parts, to be dealt with under clause 59(3) of the Conditions of Contract.

4.80 The above is certainly not meant to be exhaustive of the circumstances for all kinds of valid missing/omitted item claims and the full circumstances of any individual case need to be reviewed to see whether, and if so how far, this general principle is applicable. This is just one view for consideration in appropriate circumstances.

Considerations When Issuing Certificate and Assessing Contractual Entitlement

4.81 When deciding whether to issue the certificate, the engineer must exercise due care and skill and must act in a fair and unbiased manner: see the House of Lords' decision in *Sutcliffe v Thackrah*.[35] The engineer has to maintain the 'balance between the client and the contractor'.

4.82 For instance, the guiding principle for the assessment of entitlement for the extension of time for completion (EOT) by the engineer is what is considered fair and lawful. As noted in *John Barker Construction Ltd v London Portman Hotel Ltd*,[36] under a JCT standard form of contract, in determining a fair and reasonable extension of time there was implicitly an obligation on the architect to act lawfully and fairly. Here, 'lawful' means acting

35. [1974] AC 727 at 737.
36. (1996) 83 BLR 31.

within his power and properly directing himself as to the terms of the contract.

4.83 In *Balfour Beatty Building Ltd v Chestermount Properties Ltd*,[37] Colman J expressed the view that: 'In each case it is for the architect exercising his powers under clause 25.3.3 to decide whether an adjustment of the completion date is fair and reasonable having regard to the incidence of relevant events'. In this case, in relation to a JCT standard form of contract, in rejecting the argument that the entitlement to the extension of time in relation to instructed variations should be based on a 'gross' basis (i.e. by adding the time required for the execution of the additional works on to the date on which these works were instructed), it was held that the appropriate method of extending time was the 'net' method (i.e. the architect should start with the existing completion date and postpone it to the extent which he considered fair and reasonable having regard to the delay caused by the requirement to execute the variation instructions).

4.84 In *Henry Boot Construction (UK) Ltd v Malmaison Hotel (Manchester) Ltd*,[38] Dyson J said:

> It seems to me that it is a question of fact in any given case whether a relevant event has caused or is likely to cause delay to the works beyond the completion date in the sense described by Colman J in the Balfour Beatty case. In the present case, the respondent has what [she] calls both a negative and a positive defence to the EOT/I claim. The negative defence amounts to saying that the variations and late information etc relied on by the claimant did not cause any delay because the activities were not on the critical path, and on that account did not cause delay. The positive defence is that the true cause of the delay was other matters, which were not relevant events, and for which the contractor was responsible. In my view, the respondent is entitled to advance these other matters by way of defence to the EOT/I claim. It is entitled to say (a) the alleged relevant event was not likely to or did not cause delay e.g., because the items of work affected were not on the critical path, and (b) the true cause of the admitted delay in respect of which the claim for an extension of time is advanced was something else. The positive case in (b) supports and fortifies the denial in (a). The respondent could limit its defence to the claim by relying on (a), but in my view there is nothing in cl. 25 which obliges it to do so. Likewise, when considering the matter under the contract, the architect may feel that he can decide the issue on a limited basis, or he may feel that he needs to go further, and consider whether a provisional view reached on that basis of one set of facts is supported by findings on other issues. It is impossible to lay down hard and fast rules. In my judgment it is incorrect to say that, as a matter of construction of clause

37. (1993) 62 BLR 1 at 34.
38. (1999) 70 Con LR 32 at para. 15.

25 when deciding whether a relevant event is likely to cause or has caused delay, the architect may not consider the impact on progress and completion of other events.

4.85 It was accepted by Dyson J that the effect of other events could be considered when determining whether a relevant event was likely to cause delay beyond the completion date.

4.86 In answering this question of fact, while a formal critical path analysis is not always essential, in *Royal Brompton Hospital NHS Trust v Hammond (No 6)*[39] it was observed by Seymour J that:

> [T]here are a number of established ways in which a person who wishes to assess whether a particular event has or has not affected the progress of construction work can seek to do that. Because the construction of a modern building, other than one of the most basic type, involves the carrying out of a series of operations, some of which, possibly, can be undertaken at the same time as some of the others, but many of which can only be carried out in a sequence, it may well not be immediately obvious which operations impact upon which other operations. In order to make an assessment of whether a particular occurrence has affected the ultimate completion of the work, rather than just a particular operation it is desirable to consider what operations, at the time the event with one is concerned happens, are critical to the forward progress of the work as a whole . . . the establishment of the critical path of a particular construction project can itself be a difficult task if one does not know how the contractor planned the job. Not only that, but the critical path may well change during the course of the works, and almost certainly will do if the progress of the works is affected by some unforeseen event.
>
> [T]he various different methods of making an assessment of the impact of unforeseen occurrences upon the progress of construction works are likely to produce different results, perhaps dramatically different results . . . [T]he accuracy of any of the methods in common use critically depends upon the quality of the information upon which the assessment exercise was based . . .
>
> [I]t seemed to me . . . the making of assessments of whether a contractor was entitled to an extension of time for the completion of works on account of the occurrence of a Relevant Event as defined in the Standard Form did not depend upon any sort of scientific evaluation of any particular type of material, but simply upon impression formed on the basis of previous experience.

39. (2000) 76 Con LR 148 at para. 32.

EOT and Concurrent Delays

4.87 Concurrent delay can be defined as a period of project overrun which is caused by two or more effective causes of delay which are of approximately equal causative potency.[40]

4.88 *Society of Construction Law Delay and Disruption Protocol*[41] sets out how 'concurrent delay' can occur as follows:

> True concurrent delay is the occurrence of two or more delay events at the same time, one an Employer Risk Event, the other a Contractor Risk Event, and the effects of which are felt at the same time. For concurrent delay to exist, each of the Employer Risk Event and the Contractor Risk Event must be an effective cause of Delay to Completion (i.e., the delays must both affect the critical path). Where Contractor Delay to completion occurs or has an effect concurrently with Employer Delay to Completion, the Contractor's concurrent delay should not reduce any EOT due.

4.89 Various other definitions for 'concurrent delay' have been postulated. In *Delay and Disruption Claims in Construction: A Practical Approach*,[42] published by ICE Publishing, it is said that:

> In certain instances, concurrent delays can occur. This is a situation where two (or more) delay events have an impact on the critical path to completion at the same time.

4.90 In *Construction Delays: Extension of Time and Prolongation Claims* concurrent delays are defined to be 'delay situations when two or more delays, regardless of the type, occur at the same time or overlap to some degree—either of which occurring alone would have affected the project completion date'.[43] The text also stresses that:

> It is important to differentiate between the delaying event or cause and the delay itself. It is generally recognized that there are times when there are delays which may result from different causes, but that sometimes the causes will run at the same time or overlap . . .
>
> In analysing concurrent delays, each delay should be assessed separately and its impact on other activities and the project date for completion calculated.

40. Stephen Furst and Sir Vivian Ramsey, *Keating on Construction Contracts*, 10th ed. (Sweet & Maxwell, 2016) at paras. 8-025 and 8-026, as replaced by its Second Cumulative Supplement.
41. *Society of Construction Law Delay and Disruption Protocol*, 2nd ed., 2017 at para. 10.
42. Ali D. Haidar and Peter Barnes, *Delay and Disruption Claims in Construction: A Practical Approach*, 2nd ed. (ICE Publishing, 2014) at para. 4.11.
43. Roger Gibson, *Construction Delays: Extension of Time and Prolongation Claims* (Routledge, 2008).

4.91 In *Liquidated Damages and Extension of Time in Construction Contracts,*[44] it is said that:

> The common meaning of concurrent is going on side by side or running together at the same time. In this sense, concurrent delay applies, when any two causes of delay overlap, to the period of overlap.
>
> The Shorter Oxford Dictionary also gives 'concurrent' a wider meaning with 'contributory cause'. It is in this sense that many difficulties arise in relation to concurrent delays. Disputes arise not so much on how long was the period of the overlap, but to what cause should it be attributed; and to what extent is it permissible to consider the knock-on effects of one delay to another.

4.92 However, it is noted in *Hudson's*[45] that:

> True or real concurrency is where two or more events occur at the same time and their respective effects or impacts extend to the same period of time. However, it is generally accepted that the occurrence of real concurrency is rare. It is considerably more likely that concurrency, when it occurs on a construction dispute, will be where events occur at different times and having differing effects but where the effects or impacts of those events overlap or operate simultaneously (at least in part).

4.93 Recently, in *North Midland Building Ltd v Cyden Homes Ltd,*[46] the English Court of Appeal said:

> 16. Although in one sense of tangential relevance to this appeal, it is also necessary to say something about concurrent delay. In *Adyard Abu Dhabi v SD Marine Services* [2011] EWHC 848 (Comm), Hamblen J (as he then was) said:
>
> "A useful working definition of concurrent delay in this context is 'a period of project overrun which is caused by two or more effective causes of delay which are of approximately equal causative potency'—see the article Concurrent Delay by John Marrin QC (2002) 18(6) Const LJ 436."
>
> Like other judges dealing with concurrency, I gratefully adopt that definition.

4.94 It has been stated in *Engineering Law and the I.C.E. Contracts:*[47]

> 1(a) Concurrent Delays. The situation where there are concurrent delays, only one of which is outside the contractor's control, is most difficult. The case may arise where the contractor due to his own

44. Brian Eggleston, *Liquidated Damages and Extension of Time in Construction Contracts* (Blackwell Scientific Publications, 2008) at para. 14.2.
45. Nicholas Dennys and Robert Clay, *Hudson's Building and Engineering Contracts*, 13th ed. (Sweet & Maxwell, 2018) at para. 6-057.
46. [2018] BLR 565.
47. Max W. Abrahamson, *Engineering Law and the I.C.E. Contracts*, 4th ed. (CRC Press, 1979) at pp. 139–140 and 370.

deficiencies is late in reaching a position to start some programmed activity, but in fact could not have started the activity earlier even if he had been ready because of delay by the engineer with some necessary drawings. It is suggested that in this sort of situation the net point is that the contractor has not in fact been held up by 'delay' outside his control, and it is immaterial that if his progress had been different, he would have been so held up. The late drawings are not an actual "cause of delay" within this clause. The contractor therefore is entitled to an extension of time only so far as the drawings are withheld past the date on which he in fact became ready for them.

The above conclusion does have the perhaps unfair result that the employer may be entitled to recover liquidated damages from the contractor for delayed completion even through the employer was not in a position to allow the contractor to complete earlier, but any other principle could lead to much confusion in substituting for an examination of whether the contractual actually was delayed by a cause beyond his control a wide-ranging examination into all events that could have caused delay had the contractor's progress been different. Of course, the contractor will be entitled to an extension if he can show that he was in a position to be ready earlier for the drawings, but delayed his progress because of advance notice that they would be late—in such a case the contractor would be wise to give notice at an early stage of his decision to take that step.

Alternatively, the contractor may say that if the employer's concurrent delay had not occurred, he would have been able, for example, to increase his resources or bring pressure on a recalcitrant sub-contractor so as to overcome the delay for which he is being held responsible. It does not seem that the mere existence of that abstract possibility is sufficient. Unless the contractor raises the issue at the time and gives evidence of readiness and ability in fact, a later argument that his delay would have been eliminated or shortened but for the employer's concurrent delay is unlikely to be believed by the engineer or an arbitrator on a claim to extension. Further discussion of this almost philosophical problem of concurrent delay will be found on p. 370 in connection with disruption claims.[48]

4.95 The article entitled 'Guidelines for schedule delay analysis' by D'Onofrio and Dale[49] introduces another concept offsetting delay. The authors distinguish between concurrent delay and offsetting delay as follows:

---

48. It has also been highlighted that: 'The thorny problem of concurrent delays has already been mentioned (above p. 139). Decided cases about similar but not identical issues in different settings are not very helpful. The general rule would seem to be on principle that if the employer's actions do not actually delay the contractor because, for example, he was not in any case ready for drawings held back or the contractor cannot prove which of several causes for only one of which the employer was responsible was the operative cause of the delay and his losses, having failed to discharge the burden of proving loss due to the action of the employer the contractor is not entitled to recover compensation from him.'
49. (2019) 35(1) Const LJ 42–59.

i. Concurrent delay

Concurrent delay occurs when delays caused by the owner and the contractor (or those for whom each is responsible) both lie on separate critical paths to the project, are independent of each other, and occur at or around the same time period. Moreover, a delay to either path of work would have independently caused a delay to project completion. Concurrent delay is typically excusable but non compensable, and each party is responsible for its own time related costs.

ii. Offsetting delay

Offsetting delay is a derivation of concurrent delay in that it offsets or nullifies contractor delay for any owner delay that would have independently caused a delay to the contract completion date but for a more critical path. Offsetting delay is delay to work that is critical but not on the longest path to completion of the work. By comparison, when unique contractual language in the contract specifications prevents the end date from being constrained (therefore preventing negative float), even a contractor delay creates float on an alternate path of work that owner delays can later absorb. The inverse situation where an owner delay occurs first chronologically followed by a contractor caused delay on an alternate path of work does not result in offsetting delay because the owner delay creates float the contractor delay can absorb; in other words, the contractor is not required to hurry up and wait.

Principles Governing 'Concurrent Delay' Situations

4.96 The legal landscape in relation to concurrent delay is complicated and the law, to say the least, is far from settled.

4.97 In the Scottish case of *City Inn Ltd v Shepherd Construction Ltd*,[50] it was remarked that, where delays occurred in the completion of works under a construction contract due to a delay in receiving architect's instructions, it was necessary to differentiate between delays caused by the lateness of the instructions and those caused by their content and, in the event of delays which were partly attributable to the fault of the contractor and partly outside the contractor's control, it was necessary to make a fair and reasonable apportionment of responsibility. Lord Drummond Young observed:

> 19. While delay for which the contractor is responsible will not preclude an extension of time based on a relevant event, the critical question will frequently, perhaps usually, be how long an extension is justified by the relevant event. In practice the various causes of delay are likely to interact in a complex manner; shortages of labour will rarely be total; some work may be possible despite inclement weather;

50. [2008] BLR 269.

and the degree to which work is affected by each of these causes may vary from day to day. Other more complex situations can easily be imagined. What is required by clause 25 is that the architect should exercise his judgment to determine the extent to which completion has been delayed by relevant events. The architect must make a determination on a fair and reasonable basis. Where there is true concurrency between a relevant event and a contractor default, in the sense that both existed simultaneously, regardless of which started first, it may be appropriate to apportion responsibility for the delay between the two causes; obviously, however, the basis for such apportionment must be fair and reasonable. Precisely what is fair and reasonable is likely to turn on the exact circumstances of the particular case. A procedure of that nature is in my opinion implicit in the wording of clause 25.3.1 and .3; both of these provisions direct the architect to give an extension of time by fixing a Completion Date that he considers to be fair and reasonable.

4.98 This has been applied in Hong Kong in *W Hing Construction Co Ltd v Boost Investments Ltd*,[51] where Deputy Judge Simon Westbrook SC remarked:

> 61. Much case law has developed on this thorny question of concurrent delay, which turns on the wording of each particular EOT clause, as well as considerations of eg what is the 'dominant' delay. The relevant case law has been helpfully reviewed by Lord Drummond Young in the recent Scottish case of *City Inn Ltd v Shepherd Construction Ltd* [2008] BLR 269 at paras. 10–21, in which he reached the following principal conclusions, with which I respectfully agree:
>
> (1) The architect ought not to assess delay using a 'coldly logical approach', but instead should use a 'practical common sense approach', bearing in mind that the overriding objective under the EOT clause is to grant a 'fair and reasonable' EOT.
>
> (2) The fact that the contractor is already in delay himself is not, in itself, a sound reason not to grant an EOT; what is fair and reasonable is a question of fact to be determined according to the judgment or discretion of the architect on the particular facts of each case.
>
> (3) Where there is true concurrency in delaying events it may, in some cases, be appropriate to apportion responsibility for the delays between the two parties so as to arrive at a fair and reasonable assessment.
>
> 62. In view of the findings which I make later on Issues 5 to 7, it is unnecessary to decide this point conclusively and I decline to do so in the context of this particular case. Suffice it to say that if called upon to decide it, my tentative view is that this instruction satisfies the requirements of GCC 23(1)(e) that 'by reason of Architect's instructions, the completion of the works is likely to be or has been delayed beyond the Date for Completion'. This belated instruction was bound to and

51. [2009] 2 HKLRD 501.

did cause serious delay to the project, such that the works could not have been completed any earlier than as certified by the Architect, so that the plaintiff is entitled to 'a fair and reasonable extension of time for completion of the Works'. The contractor was thus relieved of any responsibility he might otherwise have had for the delay, even assuming that his own works were behind programme. The EOT would thus run from 1 July 2003, albeit partly concurrent with that granted for Event 1.

4.99 In *Henry Boot Construction (UK) Ltd v Malmaison Hotel (Manchester) Ltd*,[52] the parties agreed on an approach to deal with such concurrent delay, which is seemingly endorsed by Dyson J in the judgment.[53] This was referred to in a shipbuilding contract dispute in *Adyard Abu Dhabi v SD Marine Services*,[54] in which Hamblen J quoted as good law what Dyson J said in the *Henry Boot* case.

4.100 It should be noted that this example involves a relevant event which caused a period of actual delay to the progress of the works—no work could be done for a week due to the weather. If that is established then the contractor is entitled to his extension of time even if there is another concurrent cause of that same delay. A useful working definition of concurrent delay in this context is 'a period of project overrun which is caused by two or more effective causes of delay which are of approximately equal causative potency', as given in the article 'Concurrent Delay' by John Marrin QC.[55]

4.101 This agreed approach has been set out in the more recent English case of *Walter Lilly & Co Ltd v Cyril Mackay*,[56] where Akenhead J remarked:

> 365. In the context of this contractual based approach to extension, one cannot therefore do a purely retrospective exercise. What one cannot do is to identify the last of a number of events which delayed completion and then say it was that last event at the end which caused the overall delay to the Works. One needs to consider what critically delayed the Works as they went along. For instance in this case, it would be wrong to say that the problem with the Courtyard Sliding Doors delayed the Works until it emerged as a problem in April 2008. Put another way, it did not delay the Works (if at all) until it emerged as a problem which needed to be addressed.

---

52. (1999) 70 Con LR 32.
53. At para. 13, Dyson J referred to some common ground between the parties: 'Second, it is agreed that if there are two concurrent causes of delay, one of which is a relevant event, and the other is not, then the contractor is entitled to an extension of time for the period of delay caused by the relevant event notwithstanding the concurrent effect of the other event.'
54. [2011] EWHC 848 Comm.
55. (2002) 18 Const LJ No. 6 436.
56. [2012] BLR 503. This differs from the Scottish approach highlighted in the Inner House case of *City Inn Ltd v Shepherd Construction Ltd* [2010] BLR 473.

> 366. There has been a substantial debate between the parties as to how what is called concurrent (or sometimes concurrent and co-effective) causes of delay should be dealt with. This debate is only germane where at least one of the causes of delay is a Relevant Event and the other is not. It relates to where a period of delay is found to have been caused by two factors. Of course, the debate will depend upon the contractual terms in question but most of the debate in cases in this country and elsewhere has revolved around extension of time clauses similar to those contained in Clause 25 where the Architect has to grant an extension which is 'fair and reasonable'. The two schools of thought, which currently might be described as the English and the Scottish schools, are the English approach that the Contractor is entitled to a full extension of time for the delay caused by the two or more events (provided that one of them is a Relevant Event) and the Scottish approach which is that the Contractor only gets a reasonably apportioned part of the concurrently caused delay. The Scottish Approach is highlighted in the Inner House case of *City Inn Ltd v Shepherd Construction Ltd* [2010] BLR 473.
>
> . . .
>
> 370. In any event, I am clearly of the view that, where there is an extension of time clause such as that agreed upon in this case and where delay is caused by two or more effective causes, one of which entitles the Contractor to an extension of time as being a Relevant Event, the Contractor is entitled to a full extension of time. Part of the logic of this is that many of the Relevant Events would otherwise amount to acts of prevention and that it would be wrong in principle to construe Clause 25 on the basis that the Contractor should be denied a full extension of time in those circumstances. More importantly however, there is a straight contractual interpretation of Clause 25 which points very strongly in favour of the view that, provided that the Relevant Events can be shown to have delayed the Works, the Contractor is entitled to an extension of time for the whole period of delay caused by the Relevant Events in question. There is nothing in the wording of Clause 25 which expressly suggests that there is any sort of proviso to the effect that an extension should be reduced if the causation criterion is established. The fact that the Architect has to award a 'fair and reasonable' extension does not imply that there should be some apportionment in the case of concurrent delays. The test is primarily a causation one. It therefore follows that, although of persuasive weight, the City Inn case is inapplicable within this jurisdiction.

4.102 Thus, a distinction is seemingly drawn between the grant of extension of time and the recovery of loss in a 'concurrent delay' situation. One has to fall back on what has been provided in the contract. However, in *City Inn Ltd v Shepherd Construction Ltd*,[57] an apportionment approach was adopted.

57. [2008] BLR 269.

According to this approach, where there are concurrent causes of delay, none of which can be described as dominant, the delay should be apportioned as between the relevant events and the contractor's risk events.[58] It was considered that the exercise of apportionment was similar to apportionment of liability on account of contributory negligence or contribution among joint wrongdoers. Thus, on this approach, account should be taken of relative culpability in the cause of delay and the significance of each of the factors in causing delay. This represents a departure from previous authorities for apportionment in different circumstances and much weight has been placed on the words 'fair and reasonable' in relation to the wide discretion that could be made use of. With this approach, reliance on a proper construction of the contract may not be necessary as the express wording is normally silent on relative culpability.

4.103 In this regard, *Keating on Construction Contracts* states:[59]

> [W]here there are concurrent causes of delay (one the responsibility of the contractor and the other of the employer) the contractor may be entitled to an extension of time. In contrast, a contractor will normally not be entitled to receive payment for loss and expense in respect of a relevant matter in such circumstances. The fact that the works would have been delayed in any event by the concurrent delay event which is the contractor's responsibility probably does not deprive it of an extension of time entitlement in light of the Malmaison approach summarized above, but the fact that the 'but for' test of causation cannot be satisfied in these circumstances is normally taken to deprive the contractor of a loss and expense claim in respect of the relevant matter. The proper analysis of entitlement to extension of time and any associated loss and expense in each case must involve a careful consideration of the wording of the relevant clauses and an assessment of the (possibly different) tests of causation that should be applied to them in order for the contractor's actual entitlement to be arrived at.

4.104 At footnote 109 thereto, it states:

> See now *Walter Lily & Co Ltd v DMW Development Ltd* [2012] EWHC 1773 (TCC), [2012] BLR 503 where it was held that: (i) under the JCT extension of time clause wording and similar forms of construction contracts, as long as it is established that the relevant event relied upon as the basis of an extension of time claim is at least a concurrent cause of actual delay to the completion date of the works, the contractor will be entitled to an extension of time; and (ii) the approach of the Scottish Courts in this situation to permit an apportionment of the relevant

58. This is said to be justified by clause 25 of the JCT 1980 Standard Form of Building Contract where the architect is required to fix such new completion date as he considers to be 'fair and reasonable' in the circumstances. It is said that this requires the architect to look at the various events causing delay using a fairly broad approach.

59. Stephen Furst and Sir Vivian Ramsey, *Keating on Construction Contracts*, 10th ed. (Sweet & Maxwell, 2016) at para. 8-027.

period of delay between the parties so as to permit a partial award of an extension of time to the contractor probably does not reflect the law of England (see [262]–[370]).

4.105 As regards the associated loss and expense in such situations, *Keating on Construction Contracts* discusses various approaches in the context of the 'but-for' test, such as the 'burden of proof' approach, the 'Devlin' approach, the 'dominant cause' approach, the 'Malmaison' approach and the 'apportionment approach'. It summarises the position as follows:[60]

> In respect of claims under the contract:
>
> (i) depending upon the precise wording of the contract a contractor is probably entitled to an extension of time if the event relied upon was an effective cause of delay event if there was another concurrent cause of the same delay in respect of which the contractor was contractually responsible; and
>
> (ii) depending upon the precise wording of the contract a contractor is only entitled to recover loss and expense where it satisfies the "but for" test. Thus, even if the event relied upon was the dominant cause of the loss, the contractor will fail if there was another cause of that loss for which the contractor was contractually responsible.
>
> In respect of claims for breach of contract:
>
> (iii) in general a claimant will have to show that "but for" the matter relied upon it would not have suffered the loss and the matter relied upon was an effective cause of the loss;
>
> (iv) where however the loss was caused by two or more defendants then the "but for" test does not have to be satisfied, at least as regards each defendant, however each defendant's breach must have been an effective cause of the loss; and
>
> (v) where the loss was caused both by the claimant and the defendant then unless the claimant can establish the defendant's breach was the dominant cause or the defendant can show that the claimant's breach was the dominant cause, it is probable that the claimant's claim and any counterclaim by the defendant would fail.

4.106 In *De Beers UK Ltd v Atos Origin IT Services UK Ltd*,[61] Edwards-Stuart J states:

> The general rule in construction and engineering cases is that where there is concurrent delay to completion by matters for which both employer and contractor are responsible, the contractor is entitled to an extension of time but he cannot recover in respect of the loss caused by the delay.

60. Stephen Furst and Sir Vivian Ramsey, *Keating on Construction Contracts*, 10th ed. (Sweet 7 Maxwell, 2016) at paras. 9-092 to 9-098 and 9-102 and 9-103.
61. [2011] BLR 274 at para. 177.

4.107 This 'general rule' as regards the non-recovery of loss and expense for 'concurrent delays' is in line with the suggested as postulated in the paper by John Marrin QC, 'Concurrent Delay Revisited',[62] and coincides with the preference of those who drew up the *Society of Construction Law Delay and Disruption Protocol*, where it is stated:

> [Core Principle] 14. Concurrent delay—effect on entitlement to compensation for prolongation
>
> Where Employer Delay to Completion and Contractor Delay to Completion are concurrent and, as a result of that delay the Contractor incurs additional costs, then the Contractor should only recover compensation if it is able to separate the additional costs caused by the Employer Delay from those caused by the Contractor Delay. If it would have incurred the additional costs in any event as a result of Contractor Delay, the Contractor will not be entitled to recover those additional costs.

4.108 In *Royal Brompton Hospital NHS Trust v Hammond (No 6)*,[63] Judge Seymour highlighted the importance of distinguishing this with situations where the completion of the works has not been or is not likely to be delayed by the relevant event for granting EOT. He said:

> However, it is, I think, necessary to be clear what one means by events operating concurrently. It does not mean, in my judgment, a situation in which, work already being delayed, let it be supposed, because the contractor has had difficulty in obtaining sufficient labour, an event occurs which is a Relevant Event and which, had the contractor not been delayed, would have caused him to be delayed, but which in fact, by reason of the existing delay, made no difference. In such a situation although there is a Relevant Event, 'the completion of the Works is [not] likely to be delayed thereby beyond the Completion Date.'
>
> The Relevant Event simply has no effect upon the completion date. This situation obviously needs to be distinguished from a situation in which, as it were, the works are proceeding in a regular fashion and on programme, when two things happen, either of which, had it happened on its own, would have caused delay, and one is a Relevant Event, while the other is not. In such circumstances there is a real concurrency of causes of the delay. It was circumstances such as these that Dyson J. was concerned with in the passage from his judgment in *Henry Boot Construction (UK) Ltd v Malmaison Hotel (Manchester) Ltd* at paragraph 13 on page 37 of the report which Mr Taverner drew to my notice. Dyson J. adopted the same approach as that which seems to me to be appropriate to the first type of factual situation which I have postulated when he said, at paragraph 15 on page 38 of the report:–

62. John Marrin QC, 'Concurrent Delay Revisited' (Society of Construction Law UK, Feb 2013), paper 179.
63. (2000) 76 Con LR 131 at para. 31.

> 'It seems to me that it is a question of fact in any case whether a relevant event has caused or is likely to cause delay to the works beyond the completion date in the sense described by Colman J in the *Balfour Beatty* case.'

4.109 Therefore, some working propositions may be formulated.

(a) Concurrent delay may be defined as 'a period of project overrun which is caused by two or more effective causes of delay which are of approximately equal causative potency'.

(b) True or real concurrency is where two or more events occur at the same time and their respective effects or impacts extend to the same period of time. Only in exceptional factual situations is a true concurrency of this kind likely to occur. More often, it happens that the effects or impacts of such events overlap or operate simultaneously (at least in part).

(c) To be effective causes of delay, each delay resulting from individual events must be one that affects or impacts on the critical path to the completion of the works.

(d) In assessing the causative potency, judgment with reference to common sense and professional experience may be called for. Where there are two competing effective causes of delay, they often differ in terms of their causative potency.

(e) The focus is on the point in time at which such delay impinges on the progress of the works in issue.

(f) As with other EOT assessment, while each of the events of delay should be considered in isolation to see its effect/impact on the critical path, it may not be unreasonable to take into account the effects of other events known.

4.110 On the point of responsive duty on the part of a contractor faced with an entitled extension of time to complete, akin to the situation of a duty to mitigate, the contractor is sometimes obliged and sometimes entitled to re-arrange its resources/works sequences in the circumstances.

4.111 The *Society of Construction Law Delay and Disruption Protocol* Core Principle 15 states:

> 15. Mitigation of delay and mitigation of loss
>
> The Contractor has a general duty to mitigate the effect on its works of Employer Risk Events. Subject to express contract wording or agreement to the contrary, the duty to mitigate does not extend to requiring the Contractor to add extra resources or to work outside its planned working hours. The Contractor's duty to mitigate its loss has two aspects: first, the Contractor must take reasonable steps to minimise

its loss; and secondly, the Contractor must not take unreasonable steps that increase its loss.

4.112 In *British Westinghouse Electric and Manufacturing Co Ltd v Underground Electric Railways Co of London Ltd*,[64] Viscount Haldane LC said:

> The fundamental basis is thus compensation for pecuniary loss naturally flowing from the breach; but this first principle is qualified by a second, which imposes on a plaintiff the duty of taking all reasonable steps to mitigate the loss consequent on the breach.

4.113 In *Linklaters Business Services v Sir Robert McAlpine Ltd*,[65] the principles were summarised as follows:

> 131 One can bring together all these various strands in the context of this particular case as follows:
>
> . . .
>
> (e) The claimant has a duty to mitigate its loss; it is not a heavy duty and in all or most cases the duty is not to act unreasonably in the context of incurring loss. The burden of proving a breach is on the defendant which must show that the claimant acted unreasonably.
>
> (f) Every case depends on its facts but in considering reasonableness the Court needs to look at all the facts and in particular the circumstances in which the innocent claimant finds itself at the time when it commits itself to a particular remedial course of action.

4.114 Thus, as pointed out in 'Guidelines for schedule delay analysis' by D'Onofrio and Dale:[66]

> The contractor has the right to make up its own lost time on the project or complete the work more quickly than planned. Because liquidated damages are not charged until after the expiration of contract time, negative float in the schedule only becomes a breach of contract if not mitigated. The contractor may accelerate its own work to make up time in the schedule or resequencing the work to make up time. The contractor typically has a duty to mitigate delay if possible, regardless of cause, often through resequencing the schedule where possible. However, the contractor may incur additional costs as a result of resequencing, depending on the availability of labour, material, and equipment which can make the resequencing a type of acceleration.

64. [1912] AC 673 at 688–689.
65. (2010) 133 Con LR 211.
66. (2019) 35(1) Const LJ 42–59.

Other Documents

4.115 The tender, invitation to tender and correspondences may be incorporated into and form part of the construction contract.[67] Further discussion can be found in Chapter 3.

67. Stephen Furst and Sir Vivian Ramsey, *Keating on Construction Contracts*, 10th ed. (Sweet & Maxwell, 2016) at para. 1-022.

5
Contract Drafting Techniques and Common Mistakes

Ronald Pang

Overview

5.1 In the construction industry, for one reason or another, parties often fail to fully appreciate the importance of good contract drafting. Instead, they spend millions of dollars on resolving disputes, engaging lawyers and dispute resolution professionals, when many issues could have been readily avoided if they had ensured the initial drafting of the contract was done in a proper and effective manner.

5.2 However, it is important to bear in mind that there is no such thing as a perfectly drafted or absolutely dispute-proof contract. Each contract may have its own issues and uncertainties. As Lord Carnwath said, in the English Supreme Court decision in *Arnold v Britton*,[1] '[a]s Tolstoy said of unhappy families, every ill-drafted contract is ill-drafted "in its own way"'.

5.3 This chapter discusses the important elements of a contract that parties should bear in mind when embarking upon drafting. It seeks to help them make use of good drafting techniques and provide guidance to better ensure that the contract is sound and reflects the true intention of the parties.

5.4 Certain drafting techniques that are commonly used by contract drafters to avoid pitfalls are also examined and illustrated, and common mistakes highlighted.

Contract Drafting Techniques

Use of checklists

5.5 Like many professionals, contract drafters, including those in construction, are strangely averse to the use of checklists. However, time and time

---

1. [2015] UKSC 36 at para. 108.

again, it has been shown that in almost any industry the use of checklists helps reduce the number of mistakes by a considerable margin.

5.6 For example, aviation professionals have been using checklists since the 1930s and are adamant as to their usefulness. One of the perhaps best examples of the use of checklists is the pre-flight checklists used by pilots of B-17 Bombers in World War II, which reportedly allowed pilots to fly the bombers in hundreds and thousands of missions without accidents.

5.7 When properly used, checklists can reduce mistakes in contract drafting to a minimum while taking very little time to complete.

5.8 To ensure that each contract has been properly checked and vetted, it is best to include a checklist with each contract and to ensure that it has been properly completed before allowing the contract to be sent for endorsing or signing.

5.9 The elements that should be included on a contract checklist will depend on the individual, specific contract or project. However, a good starting point is as follows:

- Are the names of the parties correct?
- Have the addresses and other places been cross-referenced?
- Has spelling and grammar been checked?
- Are there any definitions undefined and are definitions consistent throughout the documents?
- Are the documents or drawings referred to in the contract all included as appendices or attachments? Are they coloured or black and white as required?
- Is the version to be executed and signed the final version of the contract?
- Are there any boilerplate clauses included in the contract? If so, have they been tailored to the parties and the contract?
- Is a dispute resolution clause included in the contract? If so, is it operative to match the needs of the parties?
- When is the date of execution of the contract? Are there any parts of the contract that will be or have been executed prior to or after the contract? Have these been explained or provided for in the contract?
- Are there any works that were commenced prior to the signing of the contract? Are these addressed in the operative parts of the contract?

5.10 In this book we cannot provide a one-size-fits-all checklist. The complicated nature of construction contracts will inevitably lead to checklists which are somewhat cumbersome. However, the careful development and implementation of checklists should pay significant dividends.

Use of headings

5.11 In some construction subcontracts, parties do not use boilerplate or *pro forma* contracts and instead rely on short form contracts that incorporate the main contract text and have reference to other documents intended to be incorporated. At the other end of the spectrum, there is also a reliance on outdated or overly complicated *pro forma* contracts which results in its own set of problems, but this is a matter for another section.

5.12 As it will be shown below, the use of short form contracts creates confusion and issues over whether and what clauses should be incorporated.

5.13 More importantly, short form contracts are hard to read due to the way they are normally drafted. They are usually drafted in a few paragraphs and commonly in the form of a quotation and a letter of intent or a letter of award. These rarely contain all the necessary terms to properly protect the parties' interest and to fully cater for all situations that may arise. Without checking for inconsistences with all the other documents intended to be incorporated or referred to, arguments over discrepancy or ambiguity may surface later. Worse still, some short form contracts make reference to or incorporate other documents that the contract drafters may not have fully or ever read through.

5.14 The documents that are referenced or incorporated are sometimes inconsistent or completely at odds with the short form contracts. In some cases, for example, there are clauses in the referenced or incorporated documents that expressly prohibit incorporation by reference.

5.15 It is understood that in smaller projects contractors and subcontractors may not have the resources or time to prepare a comprehensive contract. In such cases, it is recommended that important terms are mapped out using headings.

5.16 By adopting the usage of headings, it can at least be ensured that the most important terms are catered for within the contract. For example, a heading of 'Payment Terms', an area of utmost importance to almost any contract, will ensure that the appropriate thought and care is given to this term.

5.17 Headings also allow third parties to examine the contract in an efficient manner by letting them see what is contained in the contract from a bird's eye view and to be quickly able to focus on the important aspects.

5.18 Further, when used appropriately with word processing software, headings allow quick access to the relevant parts, particularly when coupled with search and find functions in word processing software.

Use of technology

5.19 This is now a world where most if not all parties have access to word processing capabilities, which allow for complex contractual documents to be handled easily and quickly, at least relative to the past.

5.20 In particular, typical word processing software contains many useful functions that should be put to use by every professional, whenever contracting drafting forms part of their workflow or forms a major part of their duties. Coupled with optical character recognition technologies, documents that were not searchable in the past are now more easily put to editing and checking.

5.21 Aside from more commonly used tools such as word proofing, word counting, and find-and-replace tools, there are many less commonly used features that should form part of one's repertoire.

5.22 The one feature that is used most frequently is the navigation pane which allows for the drafter to quickly move back and forth in a complex contract. By using heading styles, the software will automatically generate a navigation pane that will list out the document's contents by each various heading style. This not only allows the contract drafter to navigate the document quickly but also allows the contract drafter to reorganise the document as seen fit and to move large and small sections of the document quickly within the context of the rest of the document.

5.23 In addition, the use of headings allow the contract drafter to utilise the automatic table-of-contents generator to produce (and to automatically update) a table of contents with a click of a button.

5.24 The second feature, which is rarely used but invaluable, is the cross-reference tool, which allows the contract drafter to cross-reference paragraphs within the document. This function also highlights to the contract drafter if a cross-referenced paragraph has gone missing or is errant. More importantly, the cross-reference will be automatically updated if the underlying reference text itself is changed. For example, if one refers to (say) paragraph 4 of a document but subsequently change paragraph 4 to (say) paragraph 23, the reference will automatically change the number to paragraph 23 instead of paragraph 4.

5.25 The use of cross-referencing and macros in documents allows for other documents to be referenced or incorporated. This can be achieved using bookmarks and field text. Not only will this save a significant amount of time, but this cross-reference tool also allows for the document to automatically update when the referenced document has been changed. A good example is addresses or boilerplate clauses which are repeated in multiple documents.

5.26 Then there is the use of the cloud storage and other document sharing tools. Such tools allow documents to be accessed anywhere and allow for consistency when dealing with drafts, particularly when there are multiple drafters involved. In the past, as a result of human error, disputes have arisen over the wrong 'final' draft being engrossed for signing or last-minute changes being added to drafts. With this, the risk is reduced provided that synchronising of the cloud drive in the various devices of the contract drafters is ensured.

5.27 Lastly, before executing a contract, one should always use the compare function to see whether any change has been implemented that was not discussed before. The compare function will highlight any additions, modifications or deletions. There are some contract drafters that ignore the use of compare functions and merely rely on tracked changes. This sometimes can be unreliable and inconsistent as it does not show changes where track changes has been turned off or where changes have been accepted.

5.28 There are also extensions or add-ons that have been created to assist contract drafters, which streamline the drafting process by providing powerful tools that allow the drafter to ensure that terms have been properly defined, to allow for cross references, and to track appendices and annexes. These extensions or add-ons, while normally requiring extra payment, can be quite invaluable tools in a contract drafter's arsenal.

5.29 In addition to the above word processing tools, there is also the advent of machine learning and artificial intelligence (AI) being incorporated into contracts. Even in its relatively infancy, AI has made its mark in contract drafting, being used to check for inconsistencies within a contract, to highlight problematic areas within a contract, and to reduce errors and areas of disputes.

5.30 Another area where technology can assist contract drafters and reduce disputes is the use of building information modelling within a contract. There is no reason why such modelling cannot be referenced within the contract so as to provide clarity to stakeholders that mere specifications and drawings cannot provide on paper.

5.31 In addition to AI, there is the advent of smart contracts that utilise blockchain technology. Contract professionals should explore such smart contracts and see how they can be incorporated in their everyday workflow. In essence, smart contracts are contracts with built in algorithms that are executed at a specified event or time. Even at a glance, one can see how such smart contracts can assist contract professionals. One example relates to conditions precedent. A smart contract can be coded to detect incidents that require conditions precedent, such as applications for extension of time or assessment of liquidated damages, which usually require certain steps to be taken before they can be properly invoked, and a smart contract can notify users that such steps have or have not been taken.

5.32 It is important to bear in mind that the use of technology can lead to its own problems. For example, there can be issues with privacy, susceptibility to hacking or social engineering, as well as storage limitation issues. There is also, of course, the familiar problem of over-reliance on technology.

Use of simple language and jargon

5.33 Many drafters habitually use archaic language and jargon when drafting contracts.

5.34 Words like 'forthwith', 'furnish', 'hereinafter' and 'determine' are examples of such archaic and outdated language. These words are extremely common in contracts, despite the fact that they are rarely used in spoken English and rarely in any reasonable person's vernacular; instead, words such as 'immediately', 'provide', 'below', and 'decide' should be used.

5.35 The persistence of archaic language seems to stem from two sources. First, the extensive use of precedents and *pro forma* contracts. There has been much reliance placed on them without proper understanding of the context and the situation these precedents and *pro forma* contracts are dealing with and addressing. Contract drafters often adopt the tone and style found in such precedents and *pro forma* contracts without being recognising that the tone and style is inappropriate in context. The sort of language used in precedents or sample forms recurs in new contracts as it is difficult to change the language and tone of precedents or forms.

5.36 Second, most legal systems rely on archaic language out of tradition and for historical reasons, particularly legal systems that adopt a case law system in which law is determined or declared through adjudication of past events. As a result of this, legal practitioners and contract drafters, out of prudence and conservatism, will be slow to lead change if it is yet to be adjudicated by the legal system. However, the lack of progress in this regard can be risky in itself as language continues to evolve, leading some jargon and archaic language to lose its initial meaning. This creates issues for interpretation.

5.37 While jargon and archaic language has its place in certain situations, one can appreciate the difficulties that such language can pose when one considers that to properly understand the content of such a contract, one must learn how to read it, which is seemingly contrary to the principles behind a contract based on a meeting of the parties' minds.

5.38 Additionally, using words that are not a common part of a person's everyday vocabulary means that, during drafting, the chances of misunderstanding the meaning of words increases. No one would choose to draft a contract using a foreign language they were uncomfortable with. As such, there is no reason for a person to include in a contract words that they rarely use and are unfamiliar with.

5.39 While in some cases archaic language and jargon may be suitable, it is important for the contract drafter to review the matter critically and see whether the word is used properly to reflect the intended meaning or if it is needed as there is a law governing its use.

5.40 Contract drafters also have a common habit of using pairs of words that have substantially the same meaning instead of simply using one word. For example, 'save and except' and 'sell and convey'. It is clear that many drafters do not understand the reason to pair such words and merely do so out of habit. In fact, the reason is historical and dates back to the time when England was using two different legal systems at the same time, common law and equity. Nowadays, a 'combined' legal system is essentially in place, which means that the pairing of words is redundant but persists because contract drafters maintain old habits out of fear of being misinterpreted. The result is the contract becoming verbose, which increases the chance of misinterpretation and the intended meaning being lost.

5.41 Another form of word pairing quite common to construction contracts is the use of 'and/or'. If used without good reasons, such usage unnecessarily complicates matters as it increases the number of possibilities and scenarios by a factor of two. This can be significant when a contract already attempts to cater for a large number of possibilities in a construction project.

Use of schedules and appendices

5.42 When a contract becomes too hefty, it becomes difficult to read through. To allay this issue, construction practitioners use different methods to reduce the pages of operative parts of the contract. One common method is the use of schedules and appendices.

5.43 Schedules and appendices are particularly useful when a contract contains many standard terms that are intended to be used multiple times, with minor changes or changes to the same item over and over again. For example, schedules are prevalent in sale and purchase agreements involving land as most transactions involve the same terms and the only change from transaction to transaction involves the identities of the parties and the land being sold. This is akin to the use of contract data in the NEC forms of contract in the construction industry.

5.44 Schedules and appendices allow for the operative parts of the contract to stay consistent and therefore reduce errors and possible issues arising out of multiple appearing or repeating of same text. There are particular situations specific to construction projects in which the use of schedules and appendices are desirable and sometimes invaluable, such as:

(a) detailed requirements and specifications which are referred to multiple times throughout a contract;

(b) timetables or project programmes which can be subject to change and evolve over time;

(c) detailed and complicated payment provisions;

(d) terms and conditions relevant to other parties, such as contractors, subcontractors and other specialists.

5.45 Despite this, there is a risk inherent in using schedules and appendices that certain parts of such schedules and appendices are left blank due to their voluminous nature.

5.46 For example, in the case of *Sutton Housing Partnership v Rydon Maintenance Ltd*,[2] Sutton appointed Rydon to carry out repair and maintenance works to Sutton's projects for a period of five years. The contract included performance indicators and minimum acceptable performance levels, which were clearly of importance as Rydon's entitlement to additional payments depended on meeting such factors.

5.47 However, the figures that Rydon was supposed to meet were contained in tables in schedules labelled as 'examples'. During the course of the contract, Sutton sought to terminate the contract on the basis that Rydon had failed to meet the performance indicators and performance levels. However, Rydon argued that the contract did not contain any specific levels, the tables in the contract being labelled merely as examples.

5.48 The English Court of Appeal held that the tables were not just examples but were actual figures that Rydon had to meet. In the course of the court's judgment, the principles in *Manchester Ship Canal Company Ltd v Environment Agency*,[3] *Arnold v Britton*,[4] and *Rainy Sky SA v Kookmin Bank*[5] were applied. Jackson LJ stated (at para. 53):

> [B]oth parties must have intended (and any reasonable or indeed unreasonable person standing in the shoes of either party would have intended) the contract to specify MAPs. The only place where MAPs appear is in the three so-called 'examples' in the framework. In my view, applying the approach mandated by the Supreme Court in *Rainy Sky* and *Arnold*, the contract properly construed must mean that the

2. [2017] EWCA Civ 359.
3. [2013] EWCA Civ 542.
4. [2015] AC 1619.
5. [2011] 1 WLR 2900.

MAP figures set out in examples 1, 2 and 3 are the actual MAPs for the year 2013/2014, not hypothetical MAPs by way of illustration.

5.49 This case shows that, while common sense arguably prevailed, disputes can be easily avoided by ensuring that the schedules contain the proper content which is properly labelled.

5.50 Although this issue arose from schedules and appendices, one should appreciate that issues are more likely to occur if performance indicators are included at various points throughout the contract; the chance to miss such details can only increase if they appear in the contract multiple times.

5.51 This dispute could also have been easily avoided if checklists have been used prior to the execution of the contract to check things over prior to signing, as one of the things to be checked must inevitably be the schedules.

Guidelines for revising drafts of contracts

5.52 Revision occurs after writing in the drafting process and concentrates on small-scale organisation, sentence structure, transitions, paragraphing, grammar, punctuation, etc. There are two things to remember about revision and amendments of contracts.

5.53 First, one should not revise while one writes. This slows down both the writing and the revision processes. When one is writing, one should concentrate solely on the ideas to be included in the writing, no matter how unpolished the writing may seem. The advice is to revise later.

5.54 Second, when one revises, one should do it in stages. It is exhausting and inefficient to try to revise on every level once and for all at the same time. One should use the time for revising to move from general writing problems to more specific ones.

5.55 Some further highlighted points are set out below.

<u>Accuracy</u>: No amount of readability will replace accuracy. So, make sure first to check the content of each legal point. Ask the following questions:

(a) Is the content accurately stated?

(b) Could any point be misunderstood because of ambiguity?

(c) Are irrelevant facts or other irrelevant information excluded?

(d) Are terms of art used correctly?

(e) Are key terms used correctly?

(f) Are paraphrases accurate?

(g) Are the names of parties and their status correct?

(h) Are citations accurate?

Organisation:

(a) Are paragraphs internally logical?

(b) Are there clear and precise transitions between paragraphs and sentences?

Readability:

(a) Are subjects and verbs close together?

(b) Are unnecessary modifiers eliminated?

(c) Are sentences not overly long?

(d) Are lists clearly structured?

(e) Are unnecessary prepositional phrases eliminated?

(f) Is the text generally concise?

Style:

(a) Is style consistent?

(b) Is the tone and level of formality appropriate and consistent?

Try to give each of these categories full attention for the specific amount of time that one has allocated to the task. After finishing revising, move on to polishing the draft.

Common Drafting Mistakes

Overview

5.56 In this part of the chapter, we discuss drafting mistakes in Hong Kong construction contracts that often lead to disputes.

5.57 While most of the common mistakes can be found in any type of contract, most of the examples are situated in the context of construction disputes and, in particular, with emphasis on disputes arising from scenarios where non-standard contracts are used.

Failing to understand the goal of the contract

5.58 The essence of a contract is that it reflects the parties' mutual understanding and, in the construction context, the agreed *modus operandi*. It seems that many contract drafters are so bogged down in including exceptions and provisos that they sometimes lose sight of the importance of the mutual understanding.

5.59 This is often the case for construction contracts where the contract consists of multiple documents of various natures and is drafted by various persons at different times.

5.60 This includes documents such as drawings, industrial standards and other collateral documents such as surety bonds.[6]

5.61 In addition, there is also some complacency among construction professionals in Hong Kong in respect of basic contract formation, as there is a misconception that there is an 'industry standard' for contracts or that the Hong Kong courts will readily give effect to pre-contractual negotiations or will typically find in favour of the 'little guy' in the bargain. Unfortunately, it is not always fully appreciated that the Hong Kong courts have a tendency to focus more on contemporaneous documents and that, in contractual disputes, the proper approach is to determine, objectively, what the parties intended at the inception of the contract, albeit that the contract may, in hindsight, not seem to be a 'fair bargain'. In the words of Lord Neuberger of Abbotsbury PSC in *Arnold v Britton*:[7]

> [A] court should be very slow to reject the natural meaning of a provision as correct simply because it appears to be a very imprudent term for one of the parties to have agreed, even ignoring the benefit of wisdom of hindsight. The purpose of interpretation is to identify what the parties have agreed, not what the court thinks that they should have agreed. Experience shows that it is by no means unknown for people to enter into arrangements which are ill-advised, even ignoring the benefit of wisdom of hindsight, and it is not the function of a court when interpreting an agreement to relieve a party from the consequences of his imprudence or poor advice. Accordingly, when interpreting a contract a judge should avoid rewriting it in an attempt to assist an unwise party or to penalize an astute party.

5.62 Complacency clearly leads to contractual disputes, despite the fact that the amounts at stake are usually in the tens or hundreds of millions of dollars. However, the parties either did not see the benefit or need to have the agreement reduced to writing, or were willing to use a home-made contract that did not encapsulate the essence of the agreement.[8] The pitfalls of using such a home-made contract or relying on an oral agreement will be discussed separately.

5.63 Another issue arises from a lack of understanding of the scope of the contract and the variation works that can be ordered under it. It is not uncommon for employers or main contractors to vary the contract by

6. For example, the wording of a bond affects whether the instrument is a bond on demand or otherwise; the outcome is dependent on the exact words regarding the conditions that are to be met upon presentation of the bond and it is important that these words are unambiguous. See *Kono Insurance Ltd v Tins' Industrial Co Ltd* [1988] 2 HKLR 36; *Dragages et Travaux Publics (HK) Ltd v Citystate Insurance Ltd* [2001] 1 HKC 196.
7. [2015] AC 1619 at 1628H.
8. See *Hay Design Ltd v Heng Tai Contracting (Int'l) Co Ltd* [2020] HKCFI 358; *Tactful Construction & Engineering (HK) Ltd v Univic Engineering Ltd* [2019] HKCFI 1568.

unilaterally reducing the scope of work or changing the scope without using the proper contractual mechanism, contrary to general legal principles.[9]

5.64 While the contract drafter may have ensured that the contract is easily understandable, there is still the further need to ensure that every conceivable scenario or item is included in it. The unexpected needs to be expected and provided for.

5.65 A contract drafter should:

(a) be able to create a legally binding agreement which expresses, in clear terms, the intention of the parties;

(b) through the use of clear language, provide clear steps as to how to fulfil the intention of the parties;

(c) reduce the possibility of misinterpretation or reduce the possibility that a party can retract from its promise by pointing to ambiguity or unclear language;

(d) avoid situations where part of the contract cannot be legally effective in that it is contrary to law in the governing jurisdiction.

5.66 A contract drafter who properly comprehends and performs these roles will be well positioned to draft a contract that properly reflects the intentions of the parties so as to achieve the intended outcomes.

Failure to understand the audience of the contract

5.67 Another issue that seems common among construction contract drafting is the failure to appreciate the need for an easily understandable contract that is decipherable by those who are not practising in the construction industry or are not legally trained.

5.68 For example, in the recent case of *Maeda Kensetsu Kogyo Kabushiki Kaisha also known as Maeda Corporation and China State Construction Engineering (Hong Kong) Ltd v Bauer Hong Kong Ltd*,[10] the parties were involved in a dispute involving certain measurement rules. The dispute was referred to resolution by arbitration and an interim award was rendered. There was then an application to appeal the interim award. The judge made the following comments in respect of the measurement rules:

> 28. In my respectful view, the MRs were poorly drafted. The use of technical terms adds to the difficulty in understanding them properly. Further, the similarity of some such terms gives rise to unnecessary confusion. Furthermore, various concepts are inter-related. Therefore,

---

9. See *Abbey Developments Ltd v PP Brickwork Ltd* [2003] EWHC 1987 (Technology); *Trustees of the Stratfield Saye Estate AHL Construction Ltd* [2004] EWHC 3286 (TCC).
10. [2018] HKCFI 1057.

> the lack of clarity in one concept is multiplied when a Rule, which contains a number of related concepts, is to be construed.
>
> 29. It is essential for the understanding of the MRs to have in mind not only the relevant background, but at the forefront of one's mind the works required to be carried out by Bauer under the Sub-contract, which was the purpose for which the MRs were created.

5.69 The difficulty in interpreting the contract seems to have formed part of the basis of the judge's decision to allow a partial appeal against the interim award.

5.70 This case demonstrates the importance of clarity for audiences other than the parties in contract drafting. Ultimately, the person adjudicating any dispute will be an unrelated third party who may or may not have in-depth knowledge of the factual matrix of the contract or the dispute, or how the technical side of the construction industry operates.

5.71 While it is not necessary to boil down a contract to its bare bones and over-simplify it for the benefit of an uninformed reader, it is still important to bear in mind that not all lawyers, judges or arbitrators, particularly those who are less familiar with the construction industry, possess the skills to decipher highly technical documentation.

5.72 A related issue is the increasing use of surplusage in construction contracts. This is the practice of listing or inserting all conceivable examples or scenarios, without fully understanding the legal effects or presumptions that flow from using such words. This may further hinder proper understanding of the contract.

5.73 While contract drafters may be inclined to adopt a 'torrential style' approach to drafting contracts so as to err on the safe side of caution,[11] this approach may be dangerous when dealing with non-boilerplate contracts and may bring more problems than clarity to the contract.

5.74 In particular, when a contract is drafted for a specific transaction without adopting any standard form, the presumption is that the inclusion of any surplusage has been explicitly intended, and a party will be hard-pressed to suggest that such extra words are inoperative or merely surplus.[12]

5.75 A good rule of thumb is to consider whether the use of the professional jargon reduces the word count of a sentence. If the jargon complicates and renders a sentence verbose, then it should be considered whether the word can be replaced with some other word that is more readily understood.

---

11. See *Observations of the Court in Norwich Union Life Insurance Society v British Railway Board* [1987] 2 EGLR 137 at p. 138F.
12. See *Secretary of State for Defence v Turner Estate Solutions Ltd* [2015] EWHC 1150 (TCC) at para. 62, per Coulson J), *Achieve Goal Holdings v Zhong Xin Ore Material Holdings* [2020] HKCA 51 at para. 16(6).

5.76 However, the buck does not stop with the contract drafters. It is also incumbent on the parties benefiting from the contract to clearly articulate the goals that they want to achieve through the contract.

Failing to ensure the incorporation of relevant documents and terms

5.77 Due to the voluminous nature of construction contracts, in many cases, especially for subcontractors, terms and documents are merely incorporated by reference. In particular, contractors may seek to incorporate the drawings and specifications of the main contract into the subcontracts between them and their subcontractors, so as to avoid or reduce discrepancies during construction.

5.78 In the attempt to incorporate such documents, the contract drafter will rely on sweeping and all-encompassing terms, with exceptions and provisos stated, so as to ensure that only relevant documents or terms are incorporated.

5.79 However, such sweeping and all-encompassing terms are rarely specifically tailored for the subcontract in issue and can lead to situations in which it is not clear whether some or all of such documents or some or all of such terms are indeed incorporated in the subcontract.

5.80 Further, in some situations, despite the fact that the contract specifies that certain documents or terms have been incorporated, the relevant documents or the documents containing the relevant terms have not ever been provided to the other party for inspection.

5.81 As a result, one of the common issues in construction disputes is whether certain terms or documents have been incorporated by agreement between the parties into their contract.

5.82 Ascertaining whether documents have been incorporated into the contract is of utmost importance. For example, in relation to the scope of works, many construction disputes turn on (say) the interpretation of drawings.[13]

5.83 This trend, which is likely to continue, may be due to the ready availability of information on the internet or electronic databases that can serve as precedents. It is difficult to over-emphasise the importance of written, contemporaneous documents and their roles in ascertaining whether a term has been incorporated into the contract by reference. It seems that the Hong Kong courts are slow to go against what is stated in documents that

13. In *Yau Lee Construction Company Ltd v China Steel Engineering Co Ltd & Anor* HCCT 49/2010 (unreported, 15 August 2016), the dispute revolved around a final account for works done and whether certain works were done. Mimmie Chan J was required to interpret several drawings to determine whether certain works were in accordance with such drawings.

were drafted or prepared before the parties materialised their dispute. Hong Kong courts and arbitrators have readily and repeatedly relied on what Kaplan J said in *Eu Asia Engineering Ltd v Wing Hong Contractors Ltd*:[14]

> In construction cases, as in most other cases, I attached great significance to the contemporaneous documents. These are usually prepared in good faith before a dispute has arisen or at any rate crystalized. It is a particularly devious contractor, employer or sub-contractor who systematically manufactures documents to assist in a future dispute. Fortunately, such instances are rare. I accept that once a dispute has been identified it is necessary to pay careful attention to the documents created after that time because it is only naturally that parties will reflect their grievances and justification for action taken in those documents.[15]

5.84 In *Chan Chi Lam t/a Hoi Fat Construction Co v Lam Woo Co Ltd & Anor*,[16] a dispute arose between a subcontractor and the joint venture main contractor in respect of water main works under a government contract. The main issue was whether the re-measurement clause contained in the main contract between the joint venture main contractor and the relevant governmental department was incorporated in the sub-contract between the subcontractor and the joint venture main contractor. This was despite the fact that the subcontract between the parties explicitly stated that the standard methods of measurement were to be the same as the main contract and that the bills of quantities were provisional and subject to re-measurement.

5.85 In an attempt to argue that the re-measurement clause was not incorporated in the contract or not binding upon it, the subcontractor argued that, under the relevant work orders, the rates were agreed and interim payments had been paid on such agreed rates.

5.86 It was also the subcontractor's case that it did not fully understand the related contractual documents due to lack of education. However, Mimmie Chan J considered that that the quotations appended to the work orders included provisions in Chinese that stated clearly that the orders were to be re-measured, and hence rejected this argument. The judge found against the subcontractor in respect of the incorporation of re-measurement clause.

5.87 Such a dispute could have been avoided with clearer drafting of the subcontract.

14. HCCT 16/1990 (unreported, 23 December 1991) at p. 6.
15. Cited with approval in *Hong Kong Asphalt (Green Ltd) v Sun Fook Kong (Civil) Ltd* HCCT 17/2010 (unreported, 4 July 2014); *Evergreen (FIC) Ltd v Golden Cup Industries Ltd trading as Super Star Group* [2016] 5 HKLRD 636.
16. HCCT 52/2014 (unreported, 13 March 2017).

Home-made contracts or lack of a contract

5.88 While relatively rare at the main contract level, construction contracts at the lower tiers are sometimes home-made documents. Surprisingly, it is still not uncommon that no written contracts are used.

5.89 The nature of construction works, which are time sensitive, may make the use of self-amended precedents, other home-made contracts or oral contracts attractive, particularly in cases involving piecemeal tasks or small-scale works.

5.90 However, contracts that have not been vetted by professional advisers carry commercial risks and oral contracts pose many issues. These may even be more costly down the road as disputes arise.

5.91 First, an oral contract has an element of uncertainty that is impossible to avoid. It can be difficult to ascertain where the contract begins and where it ends. In some cases, the lack of a written agreement will be so harmful that the crux of the dispute becomes whether there exists any binding agreement between the parties.

5.92 The effect of reliance on an oral contract will be unnecessary costs incurred at any trial on this one issue. This defeats the purpose of a contract, which should serve to minimise the possibility and scope of disputes.

5.93 Further, as the existence or otherwise of an agreement is by its nature a factual matter, it means that any finding will be highly dependent on whether the judge or arbitrator hearing the dispute believes the version of the facts put forward by a testifying witness.

5.94 The most important takeaway from this section is that an oral contract will make an early settlement of a dispute difficult as it makes any finding by a court or an arbitral tribunal fact sensitive and therefore eliminates the possibility of an early judgment or bifurcated arbitration.

5.95 In *Hay Design Ltd v Heng Tai Contracting (Int'l) Co Ltd*,[17] Mimmie Chan J had to deal with a trial one the preliminary issue of whether there existed an oral agreement in respect of a profit sharing arrangement for the construction of fitting-out and decoration projects that were jointly completed by the parties. The judge emphasised the lack of contemporaneous evidence as to the claimed oral agreement and dismissed the plaintiff's claim.

5.96 Notwithstanding the clear uncertainties they create, oral contracts remain at the centre of many construction disputes. For example, in *Tactful Construction & Engineering (HK) Ltd v Univic Engineering Ltd*,[18] part of the dispute revolved around the scope of works agreed based on oral agreement and various documents included in emails. In *Eternity Contracting &*

17. [2020] HKCFI 358.
18. [2019] HKCFI 1568.

Engineering Co Ltd v The Jardine Engineering Corporation Ltd,[19] the plaintiff sought to argue that there was an agreement between it and the defendant whereby the plaintiff agreed to supply labour for certain plumbing and installation works but there was no actual written contract between the parties and the plaintiff merely relied on circumstantial evidence to substantiate its claim. A similar case was *Chan Shun Kei t/a Chan Shun Kei Construction Works v Hong Kong Construction (Hong Kong) Ltd*,[20] which arose from certain road and drainage works arising out of the Tolo Highway widening project.

5.97 As to the use of contract precedents, while they are useful tools for preparing, negotiating and drafting a contract, the drafter must be vigilant to ensure that each clause, especially the often-adopted boilerplate clauses, is appropriate for the parties and in accordance with their intended agreement.

5.98 As an example, arbitration is the mechanism for dispute resolution favoured in many construction contracts, particularly for disputes between the employer and the main contractor. Most standard forms of construction contracts specifically require the parties to arbitrate their disputes instead of allowing for the parties to have the matter dealt with by litigation before courts. Yet it may be difficult to find a neutral practitioner who is able to clearly articulate why arbitration must always be the favoured dispute resolution mechanism, as compared to litigation or other alternative dispute resolution mechanisms, especially when there is no real need for the confidentiality it offers. In this respect, the trend is for construction contracts, particularly at the lower tiers of the industry, not to refer disputes to arbitration which has lost some of its lustre, in that it is not necessarily more speedy than court processes.

5.99 Not only is arbitration not always efficient or expedient, full scale construction arbitration is an inherently expensive process. Despite recent changes to the arbitral rules of the arbitration institutions in Hong Kong, the fact is that not many arbitral tribunals will deal with cases summarily or by way of an expedited procedure without the explicit agreement of both parties, in order to avoid challenges to enforceability. This in turn prohibits the cost and time efficiency that arbitration should otherwise be known for from materialising.

5.100 This is not to say that boilerplate clauses are not a useful tool or that they should be not used at all. Rather, boilerplate clauses and precedents allow for consistency and certainty as it is possible that disputes regarding the interpretation of such clauses have been previously dealt with by the courts, including clauses relating to dispute resolution, serving of notices,

19. HCCT 33/2007 (unreported, 17 November 2016).
20. HCCT 2/2011 (unreported, 7 February 2014).

terms of payments, definitions of scope of works, etc., and that their legal implications will therefore be settled.

5.101 In this respect, the Hong Kong courts readily make reference to previous relevant decisions where the clause in question is identical to or similar to the clauses in earlier decided cases.

5.102 Another reason for the practice of relying on home-made contracts or failing to actually have a written contract may be that parties, in particular in construction disputes, rely on trade practice or common understanding. This may result in a contract that is too concise or in foregoing a written one entirely. However, the law on this is quite clear. It is not easy for parties to point to the factual context or trade practice to fill in seemingly missing terms of a contract.

5.103 As stated by Kwan VP in the recent judgment of *Achieve Goal Holdings v Zhong Xin Ore Material Holdings*:[21]

> Reliance placed on commercial sense and surrounding circumstances should not be invoked to undervalue the importance of the language of the provision which is to be construed. Except in a very unusual case, the parties have control over the language they use in a contract and must have been specifically focussing on the issue covered by the provision when agreeing the wording of that provision. A court should be very slow to reject the natural meaning of a provision as correct simply because it appears to be a very imprudent term for one of the parties to have agreed, even ignoring the benefit of wisdom of hindsight. (*Arnold v Britton* at paras. 17 and 20, per Lord Neuberger of Abbotsbury, PSC)

5.104 Therefore, to rely on trade practice or common understanding is a folly and to do so may potentially lead to a contract term being interpreted by the court against the drafter of a contract.

5.105 In addition, due to the relatively small circle of construction personnel in Hong Kong, some contractors or employers seem to rely on common understanding, trade practice or some past dealing when drafting contracts. They may trust that it is not always necessary to spell out everything and to reduce it to writing, leaving out the most obvious or most important matters from their contracts. This practice may work during the good times, but not necessarily all of the time.

5.106 There are even such cases involving matters of paramount importance such as interim payment terms or extension of time clauses. It is important to bear in mind that when disputes do arise, traditions, goodwill, and common understanding are often among the first things to be thrown out. Therefore, it is important for contracts to contain everything that is necessary and not to simply rely on tradition, goodwill or past dealings,

21. [2020] HKCA 51 at para. 16(3).

common trade practice, or common understanding, to have the essential terms implied back into a contract when needed.

5.107 Depending on what the terms sought to be implied are, it may not always be easy to imply terms into a contract. The Hong Kong courts do not readily imply terms into contracts in the context of construction disputes as the parties are usually regarded as commercial entities with easy access to professional advisors bargaining at arms' length.

5.108 In the UK, the Supreme Court recently overturned a decision to find a contract incomplete and declined to imply certain terms. This is the decision of *Wells v Devani*.[22] Kitchin LJ stated in his leading judgment that:

> [T]he courts are reluctant to find an agreement is too vague or uncertain to be enforced where it is found that the parties had the intention of being contractually bound and have acted on their agreement.

5.109 While the court in *Wells v Devani* refused to imply a term, as the terms in the contract were found to be clear enough and the only sensible interpretation was to give effect to a binding term, the court did make it clear that, if it was necessary to imply a term, it would do so but only in circumstances where it was necessary to give contract business efficacy. The court would not go beyond what was necessary for that purpose.

Lack of clear acceptance of contract

5.110 More and more construction contracts are drafted and negotiated in parallel with or sometimes even after the carrying out of works on site. This is not uncommon in cases of subcontractors on site being asked to take up other works, additional or left over. This may cause more disputes to arise.

5.111 Some contractors may, in light of forthcoming deadlines and tight timetables, believe that it is manageable for the detailed terms and agreements to be negotiated after the counter-party commenced the works. While this is permissible and sometimes unavoidable, it is still important to ensure that all essential terms, such as scope of works, timelines of works and payment terms, have been properly agreed.

5.112 Failure to ensure that there is written acceptance of the essential terms will create undesirable situations where a dispute can arise and there is no contract entered into between the parties. Importantly, it will allow a defaulting party to improperly take advantages of the lack of a binding contract and to argue about what has really been agreed.

5.113 It is also good practice to ensure that an offer (or counter-offer) has a time limit for acceptance so as to avoid situations where material circumstances

22. [2019] UKSC 4.

have changed rendering the offer (or counter-offer) to be unsustainable any longer.[23]

5.114 The determination of when a contract has been agreed is often be known as the 'battle of forms' situation, as such determination will decide which 'form' of the contract constitutes the legally binding version.

5.115 In the Hong Kong construction industry, especially given the prevalence of the use of email, there has been an increasing practice of parties foregoing signatures and instead relying on performance by the parties of the offered contract as evidence that it has been accepted by conduct.

5.116 In general, when there is a 'battle of forms' situation, there is a contract as soon as the last of the forms is accepted, i.e., when it is sent over and received by a party who acts upon it without objection being taken. In practice, the difficulty is to decide which form, or which part of which form, is a term or condition of the contract. In some cases, the battle is won by the one who fires the last shot before performance. This will be the one who puts forward the latest terms and conditions if those terms and conditions are not objected to by the other party prior to the contract being performed by that other party. In such a case, the other party will be regarded as having accepted the last shot by conduct.

5.117 In some cases, however, the battle is won by the person who gets the blow in first. If the seller of goods offers to sell at a named price on the terms and conditions stated on the back of the product, and the buyer orders the product purporting to accept the offer on an order form with its own different conditions on the back, then, if the difference is so material that it would affect the price, the buyer should not be allowed to take advantage of the difference unless it draws it specifically to the attention of the seller. This is referred to as the 'last shot principle'. In *Butler Machine Tool Co Ltd v Ex-Cell-O Corp (England) Ltd*,[24] the seller offered to deliver a machine tool on condition that orders were only to be accepted on the terms set out in the quotation. The seller's terms included a price variation clause. The buyer replied with an order containing different terms but without any price variation clause. The order had a tear-off slip of acknowledgment on those terms, which acknowledgment was duly signed by the seller. Due to the buyer's delay in accepting delivery, the seller invoked the price variation clause. It was held that the buyer's reply was a counter-offer which the seller had accepted by their acknowledgment. Also, in *Oka Electronics Ltd v Manohar Chugh (t/a Electric & Electronics Industries)*,[25] the court was

23. For example, in *Aggressive Construction Company Ltd v Wai Kin Construction Ltd* [2018] HKCFI 744 one of the arguments raised by the defendant was that the plaintiff had delayed in accepting the tender offer to such a degree that the costs of labour and materials had significantly increased so as to render the tender offer unreasonable.

24. [1979] 1 All ER 965.

25. [1991] HKLY 154.

required to determine, from reviewing a series of documents and events, whether and when a valid and standing offer was accepted. What is to be looked for is the *consensus ad idem*, i.e. the true meeting of minds and consent between the parties.

5.118 Construction professionals should be mindful when negotiating a contract that a contract can be deemed to have been entered into contrary to one party's subjective intention.

5.119 In *Novus Aviation Ltd v Alubaf Arab International Bank BSC(c)*,[26] the English court held that a letter of commitment was binding despite the fact that it was not signed by one of the parties. This was notwithstanding the fact that the letter provided for counter-signing. The court held that a party could signal its acceptance of the letter by way of conduct and that signing the letter was only one way of signalling such an intention.

5.120 On the other side of the coin, in *Global Asset Capital Inc v Aabar Block SARL*,[27] the English Court of Appeal overturned a first instance decision in which it was decided that there was a concluded contract after a telephone call that followed a 'subject to contract' offer letter. This was found to be inconsistent with the parties' subsequent communications.

5.121 Hamblen LJ explained the legal principles governing how a contract could be deemed to have been accepted or made out. Recognising it was well established that the court would look at the whole course of the negotiations, and referring to *Hussey v Horne-Payne*,[28] he stated:

> 32. This is borne out by authority. For example, in *RTS Flexible Systems Ltd v Molkerei Alois Müller Gmbh & Co KG (UK Production)* [2010] UKSC 14, [2010] 1 WLR 753, at [49] Lord Clarke, giving the judgment of the Supreme Court, cited with approval a passage from Lloyd LJ's judgment in *Pagnan SpA v Feed Products Ltd* [1987] 2 Lloyd's Rep 601 in which he stated at 619:
>
> > "(1) In order to determine whether a contract has been concluded in the course of correspondence, one must first look to the correspondence as a whole . . ."
>
> Lord Clarke then commented:
>
> > "The same principles apply where, as here, one is considering whether a contract was concluded in correspondence as well as by oral communications."

5.122 As such, to ensure that a contract is not, contrary to a party's intention, wrongly deemed to have been concluded, it is important to bear the following factors in mind when negotiating or drafting a contract:

26. [2016] EWHC 1575 (Comm).
27. [2017] 4 WLR 163.
28. (1878) 4 App Cas 311.

(a) Be cognisant of the fact that contracts can be deemed to be concluded by way of conduct, including correspondence such as emails and telephone or other oral conversations;

(b) Make sure correspondence is marked with 'subject to agreement or contract' if it is not intended that the correspondence is to be treated as acceptance, and remove terms if disagreeing with or intending to oppose them;

(c) Understand that commencement of works can be treated as acceptance of an offer and, as such, refrain from commencing works or entering a project site until the contract has been agreed and signed; and

(d) Be alerted that post-acceptance negotiation or conduct may not be admissible or be treated as matters that affect the formation or terms of the contract.

Drafting terms too narrow or too wide

5.123 Another issue that a contract drafter must deal with is how to ensure that a clause or term is sufficiently wide to cover matters of concern while ensuring it is not so wide that it may be void for uncertainty or unenforceable.

5.124 In an attempt to cover all bases, a drafter may draft a clause in an open-ended way. However, this can have a debilitating effect on the clause, the term, other terms, or even the entire contract.

5.125 On the other hand, dispute resolution clauses are readily accepted in wide terms. Many such dispute resolution clauses, in particular arbitration clauses, do not merely cover disputes under the contract or during the currency of the contract but are also invoked when disputes arise after the termination of the contract,[29] or even for disputes in tort.

Over-reliance on 'subject to contract' term

5.126 From time to time, there is also over-reliance by the contract drafter on the catch-all term 'subject to contract'.

5.127 The phrase 'subject to contract' is well known in legal parlance. Once negotiations have begun 'subject to contract', that condition or qualification is carried all the way through the negotiations.[30] Parties can remove the qualification of 'subject to contract' only if they both expressly agree it should be expunged or if such agreement is necessarily to be implied.[31]

29. See *Leung Kwok Hung t/a Kaiser (M&E) Decoration Engineering Co v Johnson Controls Hong Kong Ltd* [2018] HKCFI 1500.
30. *Sherbrooke v Dipple* (1981) 41 P & CR 173.
31. *Tevanan v Norman Brett (Builders) Ltd* (1972) 223 EG 1945.

When parties start their negotiations under the umbrella of the 'subject to contract' formula, or some similar expression of intention, it is hopeless for one side or the other to say that a contract comes into existence because the parties become of one mind notwithstanding that no formal contract has been exchanged. Where formal contracts have been exchanged, the parties are inevitably of one mind at the moment before the exchange is made; but they are only of one mind on the footing that all the terms and conditions of the contract have been settled between them. The original intention still remains intact that there should be no formal contract in existence until the written contracts have been exchanged.[32]

5.128 As to the effect of the term, i.e., 'subject to contract', in the recent English case of *Joanna Properties Ltd v Moneything Capital Ltd & Anor*,[33] Metzer QC sitting as a Deputy High Court Judge summarised the principles as follows:

> 22. In *RTS Flexible Systems Ltd* the Supreme Court held that on the particular facts of that case the equivalent of a 'subject to contract' clause had indeed been waived; not least because the putative contract had been partly performed. But in terms of the general approach, Lord Clarke said at [47]:
>
> > 'We agree . . . that, in a case where a contract is being negotiated subject to contract and work begins before the formal contract is executed, it cannot be said that there will always or even usually be a contract on the terms that were agreed subject to contract. That would be too simplistic and dogmatic an approach. The court should not impose binding contracts on the parties which they have not reached. All will depend upon the circumstances.'
>
> 23. He added at [56]:
>
> > 'Whether in such a case the parties agreed to enter into a binding contract, waiving reliance on the 'subject to [written] contract' term or understanding will again depend upon all the circumstances of the case, although the cases show that the court will not lightly so hold.'
>
> 24. In *Jirehouse Capital v Beller* [2009] EWHC 2538 (Ch) Peter Smith J held that the 'subject to contract' formula had been lifted by necessary implication. In so holding he applied the principle in *Cohen v Nessdale*. Whether he was right or wrong on the facts of that case does not concern us. His decision is simply an application of the principle to particular facts.

5.129 In simple terms, the use of the phase 'subject to contract' negates a party's intention to conclude an agreement.

32. *Tevanan v Norman Brett (Builders) Ltd* (1972) 223 EG 1945.
33. [2020] EWCA Civ 1541.

5.130 However, the phrase is not sacrosanct, and its effect depends on the conduct of the parties and the nature of the agreement actually reached.

5.131 For example, in *Goodwood Investments Holdings Inc v ThyssenKrupp Industrial Solutions AG*,[34] it was held that an arbitration claim was not yet settled in the 'without prejudice' correspondence as the relevant offer was made subject to the conclusion of a formal settlement agreement and subject to approval of the board of directors.

5.132 In this case, the English court placed great emphasis on the fact that the offer was made subject to the board approval by the parties, which indicated that the party making the offer had no authority to enter into the settlement agreement. Importantly, as the board of directors was required to exercise its judgment and to make its decision independently and in the best interest of the company, the court was not willing to accept the argument that such a broad approval was a mere formality.

5.133 As it can be seen, whether the phrase 'subject to contract' has the usual effect will depend greatly on the conduct of the parties and the nature of the transaction.

5.134 In construction projects, it seems that many parties are willing, despite the use of the phrase 'subject to contract', to commence works without a formal signed contract. As the commencement of works is an important act in a construction project, it may be difficult to argue that such commencement by a contractor is not an acceptance of the then standing offer instead of pending a contract to be subsequently formally executed.

5.135 For example, in *RTS Flexible Systems v Müller*,[35] a contractor continued works following the expiry of a short form contract (described as a letter of intent contract) while the parties were negotiating the final contract. A draft contract was then agreed (subject to some points of details which, the court held, were not regarded as essential) but was never executed. The draft contract contained a counterpart clause, which provided that the contract would not become effective until the parties had executed and exchanged the counterparts. This was treated as equivalent to a 'subject to contract' provision.

5.136 In this case, the UK Supreme Court held that the parties had agreed to waive the counterpart clause in the draft contract and that there was a binding contract on those terms, rather than the more limited terms found in the short form contract.

5.137 As such it is important that the contract drafter, during negotiation and in particular when providing a draft contract to the counterpart, is not simply relying on the phase 'subject to contract' and neglecting the possibility

34. [2018] EHWC 1056 (Comm).
35. [2010] UKSC 14.

of the party being found to have accepted the draft contract by conduct. Instead, it should be ensured and made clear that the negotiations and the conduct cannot be objectively construed as acceptance of a counter-offer or the draft contract. It should be ensured that no contract is formed until the contract is properly and formally executed.

Lack of due diligence

5.138 Another common drafting issue is lack of due diligence in following through on certain terms during the lifetime of the contract after the contract has been negotiated and pending the execution of the formal contract.

5.139 This may happen at the initial stages of the contract, when there is a lack of following up regarding the finalisation of terms or documents. This is particularly so when terms are still in flex or are dependent on another event before coming into operation.

5.140 It is sometimes stipulated that certain terms of the contract are to apply with conditions, such as being subject to another contract or a future event or other conditions that may or may not materialise at a later stage.

5.141 A lack of follow up regarding these matters is concerning as quite often the contract drafter is not involved in the administration of the contract or the subsequent disputes arising at later stages. This means that the lessons of one contract may not be known to and learned by the drafters of subsequent contracts.

5.142 Another issue is the use of more than one language in a contract. The use of both Chinese and English in a contract can cause problems. For example, in *UBC (Construction) Ltd v Sung Foo Kee Ltd*,[36] there were discrepancies between the Chinese and English versions of the bills of quantities including on matters as important as the types of tiles agreed to be used. After discussions after the contract was formed in which these discrepancies were pointed out, it appeared that the parties had agreed that the Chinese version was to be operative. However, during interim payments, the English version was used. The court found that the parties had an agreement to rectify the contract and gave effect to the Chinese version.

5.143 As such, it is important that a contract drafter has an eye on not only the execution of the contract but also considers what may happen during the lifetime of the contract. It is also important to ensure that there are mechanisms in place so that, even if the drafter involved in the negotiation may not be available to assist in case of a dispute during the lifetime of the contract, there are sufficient and readily accessible records to help determine what has taken place.

36. [1993] 2 HKC 458.

6
Important Clauses in Construction Contracts

Ronald Pang

Overview

6.1 As explained in Chapter 4, *pro forma* contracts are commonly used for construction projects in an attempt to reduce uncertainty and avoid interpretation issues. That chapter discussed the different types of common construction contracts and their general forms.

6.2 This chapter will discuss specific clauses commonly found in construction contracts with reference to their legal development and recent legal authorities affecting their operation. This discussion will be placed in the context of contract negotiation, with a view to assisting construction practitioners to avoid common pitfalls.

6.3 Not all common or frequently seen clauses will be covered in this chapter. Instead, focus will be on clauses that are commonly at the epicentre of disputes between parties, whether in court or in arbitration.

What the Contract Encompasses

6.4 Before individual terms are discussed, one must begin with the contract itself. In many situations, what a contract actually encompasses is not necessarily clear, particularly in the context of construction disputes involving subcontractors or the use of non-standard forms of contracts. There may be situations where certain terms are to be subsequently agreed or drawings are subject to change. However, certainty is critical to a contract and the contract should explicitly provide for what documents are to form parts of the contract and what are not.

6.5 In particular, between main contractors and subcontractors there is a common practice where the main contractor, in the process of the subcontracting, merely asks the subcontractor to refer to the relevant portion of the main contract (sometimes excluding the bill of quantities/schedule of rates between the employer and the main contractor) as part of the agreement between the two parties, with separately agreed payment terms or sums.

6.6 However, this gives rise to inconsistencies and uncertainties. For example, what happens to terms in the subcontract that do not reconcile with the rest of the terms of the contract? How about drawings that do not relate to the specific works that are the subject of the subcontract? Such issues should be explicitly dealt with, but parties, so as to save time and cost, often rely on an all-encompassing reference or merely include a 'back-to-back' clause, i.e. a clause by which a main contractor seeks to pass its obligations and liabilities towards the employer through to its subcontractor(s).

6.7 The 'back-to-back' clause is itself problematic as it is ambiguous and can be misinterpreted.

Payment Terms

6.8 Arguably, the most important terms in a construction contract will be the payment terms, when the amount is to be paid, how interim payments are to be made, the consequences of non-payment, etc. Payment terms define the construction contract and allow it to be broadly categorised as one of three types: a lump sum contract, a measurement contract or a cost reimbursement contract, the former two being more commonly used in Hong Kong.

6.9 For the present purposes, the focus is on lump sum contracts and measurement contracts.

6.10 A lump sum contract is one whereby the parties agree that the price will be all-inclusive if the works instructed and done fall within the agreed ambit of works. On the other hand, in a measurement contract, the price is valued on an ongoing basis and will depend on the actual works done in the context of the pre-agreed bill of quantities or schedule of rates.

6.11 Disputes revolving around the nature of a contract, i.e. whether it is a lump sum contract or a measurement contract, are frequent in Hong Kong.[1] Disputes also arise over whether the works as carried out are within the ambit of a lump sum item. For example, in *Sunley Engineering & Construction Co Ltd v Ngo Kee Construction Co Ltd*,[2] where the plaintiff subcontractor claimed against the defendant contractor for some works that the plaintiff regarded as variation works under the design-and-build

---

1. See 鄺裕成經營大成工程公司 *v* 卓賢科務有限公司 [2019] HKDC 1286; *Affluent Construction Co Ltd trading as Po Lam Construction Engineering Co v Yu Cheung Yin* HCA 329/2016 (unreported, 27 June 2018); *Wai Hang Construction Co Ltd & Anor v Harvest Engineering (H.K.) Ltd* DCCJ 2363/2014 (unreported, 21 May 2018); *The I/O of Fuk Wing Building v Ma Hing Ching* DCCJ 2356/2015 (unreported, 17 July 2017); *Ho Kwai Chun t/a Multiple Design v Wong Kin Man* HCCT 44/2011 (unreported, 4 March 2014); *Sinoearn International Ltd v Hyundai CCEEC Joint Venture (A firm)* HCA 3987/2003 (unreported, 18 April 2011); *The I/O of Hip Wo House v Daily Trend Ltd & Ors* CACV113/2004 (unreported, 26 August 2008).
2. HCCT 49/2002 (unreported, 13 December 2006).

lump sum piling subcontract, it was held that the agreed lump sum in that case would just be for the works as defined, with quantities of works signed for in the bills also forming part of the contract; the subcontractor had a legitimate claim in respect of works done by them which were necessary in order to properly complete works which had been omitted from or understated in the bills of quantities.

Lump Sum Contracts

6.12 In a lump sum contract, as the contractor is contracted to complete the project for an agreed sum, it effectively prices for risks and therefore at a greater sum.

6.13 Many disputes arise from such contracts when the final cost incurred by a contractor far exceeds the agreed lump sum and the parties cannot agree on whether the contract was initially intended to be one of lump sum or one of measurement.

6.14 For example, in *Sinoearn International Ltd v Hyundai CCECC Joint Venture (A firm)*,[3] the plaintiff claimed to have been contracted to deal with precisely 6,410,770 cubic metres of contaminated mud dumped with it by the defendant. In the event, the defendant dumped a smaller quantity of the contaminated mud. The plaintiff argued that the contract was a lump sum contract, whereas the defendant contended that it was a measurement contract and consequently that it was only required to pay the plaintiff for the amount of mud actually dumped at the agreed unit price.

6.15 In dismissing the plaintiff's argument, Au J (as he then was) held:[4]

(a) there was no express term in the relevant contractual agreements as to the amount of contaminated mud purportedly agreed to be dumped;

(b) while the plaintiff's case was predicated upon the background of the case implying an agreed quantity, in particular the facts that at the inception of the agreement the parties knew how much contaminated mud existed and that the plaintiff had to incur substantial upfront costs for dumping permits, throughout the material time the parties merely had a rough estimate as to the exact quantities of mud; and

(c) the express clauses in the agreements contradicted the case that there was an agreed term as to quantity.

6.16 This case demonstrates that contractors should consider the following before agreeing to a lump sum contract:

(a) whether the costs of the labour, materials and overheads are reasonably ascertainable and will be consistent throughout the entire

3. HCA 3987/2003 (unreported, 18 April 2011).
4. Ibid., at paras. 90–104.

contract period and, if not, whether an appropriate fluctuation clause is included in the contract;

(b) that there is express wording in the final and executed agreement/ contract which specifies the amount of works to be done under the agreement/contract; and

(c) that the extent of the works required to complete the project is reasonably ascertainable from the contract documents.

6.17 The importance of ensuring that a contract is properly described as one of lump sum or measurement cannot be ignored. However, such a label is not the be-all and end-all of such disputes, as the label can only take a party's case so far as the label permits. This is highlighted in the case of *Sunley Engineering & Construction Co Ltd v Ngo Kee Construction Co Ltd.*[5] In relation to a lump-sum design-build subcontract, the defendant contended at trial that, if quantities other than those estimated in the plaintiff's schedule of rates were required, it was at the plaintiff's risk under the subcontract because it was the designer as well as the builder.[6] The judge rejected that argument and said:

> 36. This issue, ultimately, came down to one question: was Sunley obliged to take into account 'highway loadings'. Ngo Kee argue that they should have done but did not. Sunley agree that they did not but contend that they were not obliged to. If they were obliged to, a difficult and technical exercise must be embarked upon to determine the extent of and the cost of the under estimation.
>
> 37. There is no issue between the experts that there was no under estimation if Sunley's obligation was limited to (a) tendering upon the basis of the loading plans provided to them and (b) completing the works in accordance with those plans. It is a fact that the loading plans and schedules specified the gravity and wind loads only. They made no specific reference to 'highway loads'. Ngo Kee say that Sunley should have taken highway loads into account when preparing its tender. Highway loads form part of the requirements of the Buildings Department. Ngo Kee submit that Sunley was required to comply with the 'BD requirements' and accordingly provide for such loadings.
>
> 38. In my judgment the stance taken by Sunley was correct. It was consistent with their entire tendering exercise. They tendered on the basis of the information supplied. MMBP provided information for gravity

5. HCCT 49/2002 (unreported, 13 December 2006).
6. It was common ground that the subcontract was a design and build lump sum contract, which was provided at para. 5: 'the subcontract works shall be carried out and completed in accordance with the bill of quantities'. The judge took the view that it was no more than commercial common sense to construe this contract as one where the quantities signed for formed part of the contract and therefore there was a legitimate claim in respect of works done which were necessary in order to properly complete the works, which had been omitted from or understated in the bills of quantities.

loads and wind loads. Sunley tendered accordingly. Ngo Kee argue that Sunley must have known that highway loads should be involved because it was an elevated deck that was being built. However, it was perfectly possible that the highway loads had been included in the calculation of the gravity loads. MMBP did not specify. I consider Sunley's obligation was limited to designing on the basis of the figures provided and not making enquiries about what the figures did or did not include.

6.18 In most cases, as between contracting parties, there can be an inherent imbalance of bargaining power. Some parties, in particular the employer or the main contractor, may prefer the consistency and certainty that a lump sum contract may avail them when dealing with a contractor or sub-contractor, as the case may be. Whether this is effective depends on the drafting.

6.19 As a result, many construction contracts in Hong Kong are lump sum contracts, which makes it important for parties to ensure that the above considerations are taken into account or properly dealt with at the negotiation and drafting stages.

Measurement Contracts

6.20 A measurement contract is a contract whereby the amount paid under the contract will be according to the amount assessed as the works are done and completed. In essence, the final contract sum is calculated based on what is actually done and also based on a pre-agreed bill of quantities or schedule of rates.[7]

6.21 There are special considerations when a party enters into or agrees to a contract of this nature.

6.22 In some cases, despite the contract as a whole being calculated by way of measurement, there may be certain items for which payment is made on a lump sum basis. For example, while a contract may provide payment for piles to be calculated on a number of piles basis, it may not allow for payment on the basis of the length of the said piles.

6.23 In *Sam Woo Bore Pile Foundation Ltd v Chain Overseas Foundation Engineering*,[8] the plaintiff sought extra payment for toeing-in of piles on the basis that the contract was a measurement contract and construction on site was required to exceed the agreed length of toeing-in, 1.5 metres. The plaintiff relied upon a special condition in the contract which stated

7. Different considerations may arise if the measurement is based on pre-agreed bills of quantities and schedule of rates.
8. HCCT 76/1996 (unreported, 21 February 2006).

that the quantities in the tender documents were approximate figures and the exact length was not ascertainable until construction.

6.24 At the first instance, Reyes J (as he then was) rejected that argument on the basis that there was a unit rate of HK$36,000 for any additional length of the pile toeing-in past 1.5 metres. In effect, Reyes J accepted the argument of the defendant:

> The effect of [the defendant's] case is that [the plaintiff] would indeed have to bear the risk of toeing-in length being in excess of 1.5 m. As it turned out, the excess in many piles amounted to more than 5 m and on occasion came to as much as 11 m.

6.25 This decision was upheld by the Court of Appeal and a further application to have the matter heard by the Court of Final Appeal was rejected.

6.26 This authority serves to show the pitfalls of measurement contracts:

(a) despite the fact that the contract may be, on the whole, on the basis of measurement, individual items may be paid on a lump sum basis;

(b) when determining whether a specific item is paid on a lump sum basis, the court will take into account a large variety of factors and will read the contract as a whole;

(c) even if the size or length of an item, at the inception or even currency of the contract, is unknown and can only be ascertainable at the time of construction, it may still be paid on a lump sum basis if the contract provides for additional payment on a lump sum basis; and

(d) if a contractor contends that an item needs to be measured before payment, it should be slow to seek interim payment on a lump sum basis.

6.27 Further, as measurement contracts are highly dependent on the agreed rates, it is important to ensure that rates contained in bills of quantities or schedules of rates are properly agreed and priced and that they are operative during the currency of the contract. For example, a dispute arose in *Tactful Construction & Engineering (HK) Ltd v Univic Engineering Ltd*[9] whereby the defendant disputed the 'all-inclusive' rates as shown in the relevant bill of quantities despite the fact that it had not voiced any objections during any stage of the contract, even though it was clear that it had been aware of the issue all along.

6.28 The court in *Tactful Construction* placed great emphasis on the fact that the defendant did not actively seek to address its concerns that the rates in the bills of quantities were 'exceedingly high' and 'devoid of any commercial sense'. Mimmie Chan J stated (at para. 19):

9. [2019] HKCFI 1568.

> The Defendant and Counsel repeatedly stated that the rates set out in the 24/1 BQ were 'exceedingly high', such that they were said to be 'devoid of any commercial sense'. It is not the function of the court to determine the commercial attractiveness of any price in a contract which had been freely negotiated between the parties. Nor is the court in a position to judge the commercial sense of the price. There is no expert evidence on the market price prevailing then, and there may have been many commercial reasons, and quid pro quo, not in evidence, as to why the parties had negotiated and agreed on that price. *The appropriate time for the Defendant to comment and bargain with the Plaintiff on the level of pricing is the time when the Sub Contract was being negotiated*—and not at trial, after the agreement has been made and the contract work completed, and a claim is made by the Plaintiff for the price agreed. [emphasis added]

6.29 The highlighted passage shows the importance of addressing any issue as it arises. It seems to be a common practice among construction professionals to deal with issues and concerns only after the 'dust settles', which is undesirable for so many reasons, including the fact that a construction project sometimes spans decades and the parties' relationship may deteriorate during the lifetime of the project, which may make any negotiation after the events impossible.

Interim Payments Terms

6.30 One area of frequent contention in construction disputes is the terms for interim payment, cashflow being the lifeblood of a construction project.

6.31 Due to their interim nature, disputes arising from such payment terms rarely get ventilated in court proceedings or arbitration proceedings, where the focus is more often on the final account between the parties.[10] In most cases, issues stemming from interim payment terms usually arise as an afterthought.

6.32 The starting point regarding interim payments and certificates is that they are not conclusive or final unless otherwise explicitly agreed. The figures contained in such payments and certificates are meant to be provisional and represent only an approximation.[11]

6.33 As a result of their non-conclusive nature, the court can, on the facts, review interim certificates and revise them.[12]

---

10. Interim payment disputes may have an impact on the interest to be awarded in the proceedings.
11. *Beaufort Development Ltd v Gilbert-Ash Ltd* [1999] 1 AC 266; *Wide Project Construction (HK) Ltd v I/O of Yen Dack Building* HCA 3759/2002 (unreported, 3 March 2006); *Wong Chuk Kin v Millennium Engineering* HCA 876/2004 (unreported, 17 August 2007).
12. *Beaufort Development Ltd v Gilbert-Ash Ltd* [1999] 1 AC 266.

6.34 The things that need to be considered when dealing with interim payment terms are: (1) the time for payment pursuant to the relevant certificate; (2) whether materials/goods are included as part of interim payment; (3) the mechanism for recovery of interim payments whether as a whole or in part; (4) who can certify interim payment.

6.35 In respect of timing, generally speaking, once the interim payment is certified and the relevant certificate is issued, the certified sum becomes a debt and the sum is required to be paid in accordance with the time specified in the contract.

6.36 An important issue for contractors in construction projects is whether an employer can withhold payments so certified under a contract.

6.37 Unfortunately, there is no one-size-fit-all solution in this regard and it will greatly depend on the provisions and construction of the contract. Most frequently, interim payments are withheld as a result of a variety of reasons or excuses.[13]

6.38 As to the factors other than those listed in para. 6.34, those should be tailored in accordance with the needs of the parties.

Pay-When-Paid Clauses

6.39 A 'paid-when-paid' situation is where a party, for example a subcontractor, is paid when the party in the upper tier, i.e. the main contractor, is paid by the employer.[14] This is more common in situations when the subcontractor is nominated by the employer, where such a clause is commonly used.

6.40 An effect of such terms/clauses is that they distribute risks across the parties for situations where the employer may become insolvent or unable to pay.

6.41 The effect is that a main contractor will not necessarily be out of pocket as a result of payments made to the subcontractor, which makes this arrangement very attractive even in situations where a main contractor is not required to appoint a nominated subcontractor, i.e. when it is at liberty to choose its own subcontractor.

6.42 As a result, it is quite common for subcontracts to contain clauses to this effect. Contractors are fond of including a throwaway or short line describing the subcontract to be in this nature to give them some leeway when the time for interim payment arises.

13. These, for example, include the contractual arrangements for set-off and the existence of other projects between the parties in issue.
14. This is in contrast with a 'paid-if-paid' situation whereby a subcontractor is only paid if and only if the main contractor is paid by the employer.

6.43 However, a lack of proper understanding of such a clause has, on many occasions, made it difficult to enforce the 'pay-when-paid' clause as a 'pay-if-paid' clause.

6.44 When negotiating or drafting a contract that includes a 'pay-when-paid' term or that is in the nature of 'pay-when-paid' is to ensure that the wording used is sufficiently clear and obvious to give effect to that payment mode.[15]

6.45 The words must be clear to the extent that the agreed term, on the face of it, is unambiguous because 'pay-when-paid', if to be read as 'pay-if-paid', basically places a pre-condition on whether a party gets paid pursuant to the contract.[16]

6.46 Therefore, to ensure that a 'pay-when-paid' clause is effective as a 'pay-if-paid' clause, it is important for the contract drafter to ensure that the condition precedent, i.e. that payment is to be effected only after money is received from another party, is clear and explicit. What is meant by receipt of payment and how this interacts with any right to set-off are issues to be considered as well. More importantly, such clauses should be explicitly, and not merely, referred to or incorporated by reference. For example, it may be that a simple phase that the payment is 'back-to-back' is insufficiently clear to confer such an effect. Instead, for fairness and clarity, the exact timing and conditions for entitlement to payment have to be made clear, such as by stipulating that payment will be effected within a defined period and only after money is received from the employer or the upper tier contractor.

6.47 Further, it seems that if the relevant payment clause is contradictory to other clauses in the contract, the court will be slow to accept that the clause is in the nature of a 'pay-if-paid' clause in truth.

Delay/Extension of Time Clauses

6.48 Another common form of disputes arising from construction contracts relates to delay and whether an extension of time to complete should be granted.[17] This section deals with applications by a party who has caused a delay or is entitled to an extension of time.

---

15. *Kim Hung Construction & Engineering Co Ltd v Standard Refrigeration & Engineering Co Ltd* HCCT 37/2012 (unreported, 21 June 2013); *Wo Hing Engineering Ltd v Pekko Engineers Ltd* HCA 5561/1996 (unreported, 7 September 1998), *Honeywell Ltd v Kin Ming E&M Works Ltd and Anor* HCCT 76/2001 (unreported, 5 May 2004) *Massford (HK) Ltd v Wah Seng General Contractors Ltd* [2006] 1 HKC 58.
16. Per master Towle in *Smith & Smith v Winstone* [1992] NZLR 473 at page 481.
17. For example: *Chun Wo Building Construction Ltd v Metta Resources Ltd* HCCT 29/2013 (unreported, 19 August 2016); *P v C* [2019] HKCFI 2625; *N v C* [2019] HKCFI 2292; *Leighton Contractors (Asia Ltd) v Stelux Holdings Ltd* HCCT 29/2004 (unreported, 10 September 2004);

6.49 In general, a contractor is bound to complete the subject works within the agreed time or, in the absence of an agreed time, within a reasonable time.[18] In a situation where a contractor cannot complete the works in time, it may be liable to pay damages, usually in the form of liquidated damages if so agreed for.

6.50 In most construction contracts, at least those between an employer and a contractor, there will be provisions providing for what is to happen when the agreed contractual completion date cannot be met or when a situation occurs that puts the programme in jeopardy. It is important to ensure, when drafting such provisions, that the drafting is clear and concise so as to set out the mechanism and operative details as to what can be claimed or compensated, when and how such claims or compensations are required to be made, and the consequences (if any) of default in following these, so as to give certainty.

6.51 As an example, the General Conditions of Contract for Building Works[19] (GCC) provide for the following situations where extension of time to completion can be granted:

(a) delay arising from or in connection with bad weather;

(b) variation of works pursuant to the contract;

(c) increase in quantity of works;

(d) lack of possession of the construction site;

(e) disturbance of works caused by the employer or other contractor or consultant.

6.52 Situations outside those stated will not give rise to an extension of time under the contract. Although the above list of scenarios is quite extensive, it is important to note that, even with such widely drafted wording, there is no guarantee that all situations will be covered. For example, the above list does not cover situations where an addition to works falls outside the ambit of the contract.

6.53 As a contractor, it is important to ensure that the extension clause is drafted in a flexible manner to ensure that one is not unreasonably held liable for liquidated damages. On the other hand, an employer may be more concerned with limiting the possibility of a contactor being able to claim an extension of time in order to give some certainty of timely completion. A balance is needed to achieve the result that the parties intend, and it is

---

The I/O of Repulse Bay Towers v Bolton Construction Co Ltd [2003] 3 HKLRD 823; *Sunbond Engineering Ltd v Konwall Construction & Engineering Co Ltd* HCCT 15/2003 (unreported, 25 May 2004); *W Hing Construction Co Ltd v Bond Investments Ltd* [2009] 2 HKLRD 501.

18. *Charnock v Liverpool Corp* [1968] 1 WLR 1498; *SABIC UK Petrochemicals Ltd (formerly Hunstman Petrochemicals (UK) Ltd v Punj Lloyd Ltd* [2014] EWCA Civ 1288; [2014] 7 WLUK 1161.

19. 1999 ed., Clause 50(1)(b).

important to bear in mind that such a clause also serves the function of preventing the contract completion time from becoming 'at large' due to prevention of the employer.[20] Such prevention of the employer is act or omission in breach of the contract that, for example by late issuance of drawings, prevents or delays the completion of the works on the agreed completion date.

6.54 The next issue parties should be concerned with is when an extension of time application should be made and how and whether non-compliance with it bars any otherwise incurred rights to apply for or receive an extension of time.

6.55 In most cases, it is incumbent on a contractor to ensure that the process of applying for extension of time is invoked. Usually, as part of the process, the contract will require that, after an application for extension is made, the justifications and details of the delay be submitted.

6.56 What is important, at least for a contractor, is to ensure that the requirements for an application for extension of time are well set out in the contract so that, in the event that an extension of time is needed, a contractor can readily invoke the relevant clause.

6.57 In addition, there has been an evolving approach adopted by contract drafters when dealing with concurrent delay situations.[21] A concurrent cause of delay occurs when, for example, there is an incident which leads to an entitlement to grant of extension of time and another incident occurs simultaneously without entitlement. How the extension of time clause is to operate for such concurrent causes or concurrent delays needs to be approached carefully. However, at the end of the day, what the parties have agreed in the contract will usually prevail. For example, *North Midland Building Ltd v Cyden Homes Ltd*[22] involved a construction contract with a properly drafted clause that was unambiguous and, where a delay was due to the contractor, placed liability for the concurrent delay on the contractor. This meaning was upheld such that no extension of time was

---

20. This is illustrated in *AID Ltd v Nanyang Brothers Tobacco Co Ltd* DCCJ 1559/2013 & 876/2014 (unreported, 20 April 2015); DDJ LC Cheng stating at para. 64: 'the law is succinctly stated in Keating on Construction Contracts, 9th ed., paras. 8-013 to 8-014: "Time at large. Absent an effective extension of time clause and unless the contract clearly provides otherwise, an act of prevention by the employer releases the contractor from its obligation to complete the works within or by any fixed period or date. The contractor's time obligation is then considered to be 'at large' and the original obligation to complete the works by a fixed dated is replaced by an obligation to complete within a reasonable time".'
21. For details and governing legal principles, refer to cases like *Walter Lilly & Co Ltd v Giles Patrick Cyril Mackay & DMW Developments Ltd* (2012) 143 Con LR 79; [2012] EWHC 1773 (TCC) and *Henry Boot Construction (UK) Ltd v Malmaison Hotel (Manchester) Ltd* [2001] QB 388; [2000] 3 WLR 1824; [2001] 1 All ER 257.
22. [2018] BLR 565.

granted, even in the case of an equally effective cause of that delay for which the employer could be responsible.

6.58 In this respect, reference may be made with the effect of incorporating into the contract some standard protocols, such as the Society of Construction Law Delay and Disruption Protocol,[23] to expressly cater for such a situation to minimise the chance of dispute.

6.59 Such standard protocols also contain suggestions on how to specify the ambit and assessment of loss and damage suffered by a party in those situations. There is nothing to prevent the parties from agreeing on the loss and damage aspects in the case of termination or breach of the contract by adopting standard protocols on delay and disruption.

Variation Clauses

6.60 Most building contracts contain provisions that allow employers to change the scope of works or design of the works depending on the circumstances. The usual reason for the parties to include such a clause is to allow the employer or the designer flexibility to ensure that the completed works meet the project requirements. This is particularly important in a lump sum contract.

6.61 It is important to note that, without a clause giving a party the express power to order parts of the scope of works to be omitted with a consequent adjustment of the rest of the contract, a party generally has no power to vary a fixed price contract by reducing the works to be done.[24]

6.62 If there is no such provision in the contract, an employer will be in breach of contract and be liable for damages if it seeks to amend the scope of work, in particular, where the deduction of works would lead to a reduction in the contract sum.

6.63 The rationale for this is that a contract for execution of works confers not only the duty to carry out the works but also the right to be able to complete such works without interference.[25]

6.64 If a party seeks to include a clause to allow it to vary the scope of works, it must careful that the wording is wide and clear enough to cover the

23. 2nd ed., 2017: https://www.scl.org.uk/sites/default/files/documents/SCL_Delay_Protocol_2nd_Edition_Final.pdf.
24. *Tancred Arrol & Co v The Steel Co of Scotland Ltd* (1890) 15 App Case 125, *SWI Ltd v P&I Data Services* (2007) BLR 430.
25. See *Abbey Developments Ltd v PP Brickwork Ltd* [2003] EWHC 1987 (Technology) at para. 45 per HH Humprey Lloyd QC; *Trustees of The Stratfield Saye Estate v AHL Construction Ltd* (2004) EWHC 3286 (TCC).

intended variation. In this vein, the English court in *Abbey Developments Ltd v PP Brickwork Ltd*[26] stated:

> In my judgment, the answer is that the purpose of the variation's clause is to enable the employer to alter the scope of the works to meet its requirements. As a project proceeds it may become clear that some change of mind is needed to attain the result now desired. That might be a simple realization that something is no longer needed (especially if it was always an option, typically signalled by the use of a provisional sum or some other indication of a lack of commitment or by the absence of the necessary definition) or it might be for some of the reasons such as lack of money, or a change in the requirements of the actual or prospective occupier or user. The test must therefore be whether the variations clause is or is not wide enough to permit the change that was made. If, with the advantage of hindsight, it turns out that the variation was not ordered for a purpose for which the power to vary was intended then there will be a breach of contract. So the motive or reason is irrelevant; it is not necessary to embark on the uncertainties inherent in the suggestion in Hudson of 'placing a reasonableness as opposed to an exploitative interpretation of the variation power'; nor is it necessary to speculate whether this will be the occasion to reveal that the concept of good faith in all performance of the contract is (and always has been) part and parcel of English law (albeit well hidden); the test is familiar and objective—what purpose did the contract envisage? That purpose must however be expressed with clarity to displace the contractor's right to have the opportunity of completing all the work distinctly undertaken.

6.65 A poorly drafted variation clause can have serious consequences. Not only may an employer be liable for breach of contract, but the contractor may refuse to carry out works and treat the contract as repudiated. Further, the employer may be liable for any loss of profits suffered by the contractor on top of the costs of hiring another contractor to perform the variations.

6.66 In the Standard Form of Building Contract,[27] for illustration, the standard variation provisions can be found at clause 13.1:

> Architect's authority to issue instructions requiring a Variation
>
> (1) The Architect may issue an instruction requiring Variation provided that:
>
> (a) the Contractor has the right of reasonable objection to a variation which imposes or changes an obligation or restriction on the Contractor regarding access to the Site, use of any part of the Site or limitation of working space or working hours and the Architect

26. [2003] EWHC 1987 (QB) at para. 50.
27. Agreement and Schedule of Conditions of Building Contract (Standard Form of Building Contract) for Use in Hong Kong, 2005 edition with quantities and 2006 edition without quantities.

shall, upon receipt of the Contractor's objection, either confirm or withdraw the instruction and if the instruction is confirmed, the Contractor may refer the matter to arbitration under clause 41;

(b) the Contractor's written consent is given to an instruction either nominating a subcontractor to carry out work include in the Contract Bills which is to be carried out by the Contractor or omitting work in order for it to be carried out by others; and

(c) the instruction or accumulation of instructions shall not fundamentally change the scope or nature of the Works.

(2) The instruction requiring Variation shall describe the change required to the design quality or quantity of the Works or the imposition of or change to any obligation or restriction on the Contractor and where appropriate the Architect shall issue revised drawings and/or schedules.

6.67 When interpreting such a clause, the Hong Kong courts have been willing not only to take into consideration the wording of the relevant clause and the nature of the variations but also to examine these in the context of the overall objectives of the contract.[28]

Termination Clauses

6.68 Termination clauses, while of themselves not featuring in many disputes in the Hong Kong courts, give rise to one common issue in construction disputes. This is whether an employer has wrongfully terminated a contractor. Whether a contract is lawfully terminated is of great concern as this issue gives rise to other claims, such as claims for liquidated damages,[29] damages for loss of profit or non-completion, and other breaches of contract.

6.69 Despite this, standard construction contracts do not provide for many situations allowing a contractor or an employer to terminate the contract without legal consequences. Without a wide and clear termination clause, disputes and arguments inevitably follow.

---

28. See *Ipson Renovation Ltd v The I/O of Connie Towers* HCCT 26/2014 (unreported, 16 December 2016), where Mimmie Chan J found that the employer defendant was in breach of the contract by issuing variation orders to omit parts of the original scope of works. This was despite the fact that *prima facie* there was a provision to allow for ordering the omission of works. The rationale was that the variation was not made in order to complete the underlying project but instead to deviate from the needs and stated aims of the project, including the purposes of the contract.
29. See *Triple Point Technology Inc v PTT Public Company Ltd* [2021] UKSC 29, where the UK Supreme Court provided clarification on the extent to which a liability for liquidated damages could survive the termination of a contract.

6.70 For example, in *Aggressive Construction Co Ltd v Wai Kin Construction Ltd*[30] the defendant was required to perform timber formwork at various sites.

6.71 The plaintiff complained that the defendant had failed consistently to provide sufficient workforce to carry out the works and parts of the works were suspended at various times, along with threats to abandon or discontinue the contract works unless the price was revised. On this basis, the plaintiff argued that the defendant had evinced an intention not to be bound by the contract.

6.72 The plaintiff was successful, and it can be seen from the facts of the case that the conduct of the defendant was manifestly unreasonable. The defendant had committed multiple breaches of the contract, or at least had acted in a completely unacceptable manner by any professional standards. If each complaint was taken individually, it might or might not be sufficient to entitle the plaintiff to terminate the contract. Thus, like others, the plaintiff had to wait for the proverbial 'straw that broke the camel's back' before it was sufficiently confident to actually assert termination of the contract.

6.73 At the main contract level, this is usually less of an issue as there are standard clauses which allow for early termination. However, at the subcontract level, such terms and clauses are relatively rare. It is advisable for contractors to at least make reference to standard forms for guidance on this matter.

6.74 For example, clause 25 of the HKIA/RICS Standard Form of Building Contract sets out certain scenarios in which an employer can lawfully terminate a contractor. These are limited and constrained to situations that are clear cut or unequivocal. An employer is entitled to terminate the engagement of the contractor in the following situations under clause 25(1):

(a) the contractor without reasonable cause suspends the works in its entirety;

(b) the contractor fails to proceed regularly and diligently without reasonable cause; or

(c) there is a persistent refusal or neglect to comply with written notice from the architect/consultant in removing defective work or improper materials that adversely affect the works.[31]

6.75 At first blush it seems that the above situations should be sufficient to cover most if not all situations where an employer wants to terminate the

30. [2018] HKCFI 744.

31. This is based on the 1986 edition, with second amendments in July 1999, published by the Hong Kong Institute of Architects, the Royal Institution of Chartered Surveyors (Hong Kong Branch) and the Society of Builders, Hong Kong.

engagement of a contractor prior to completion of the works. However, in the attempt to encompass as many situations as possible, the clause does not offer much certainty.

6.76 This is evident by the use of the word 'reasonably', which is difficult to concisely define or to ascertain the operation of in context. This issue will eventually require adjudication and will thusly fail to achieve what the parties really want in terms of certainty. It is a fertile source of arguments.

6.77 As such, it is important for contractors and employers to properly identify what is of greatest concern to them and perhaps to include provisions in contracts to ensure that they are comfortable that they are able to invoke termination clauses when the proper situation arises.

Liquidated Damages Clauses

Present Hong Kong approach

6.78 Traditionally, a liquidated damages clause must be a genuine estimation of damages, not a penalty. This is a well-known and accepted principle. However, how it is to be determined is a difficult question of fact and law, and, over the last few years, there has been some movement away from this approach.

6.79 In summary, when a contract is breached, in particular in the case where the breach does not go to the root of the contract and hence does not entitle a party to terminate it entirely, the innocent party may sue for damages based on the actual loss suffered. These are unliquidated or general damages under common law. In order to avoid delays or arguments in determining this amount, and, as most construction contracts still require completion even with some delays, a contract may specify an amount of compensation—or 'liquidated damages'—to be paid in case of a breach so as to give the parties certainty while at the same time allowing the works to proceed and be completed.

6.80 For the past few decades, the approach of the Hong Kong courts has been that this was permissible as long as the amount is a 'genuine pre-estimate' of damages at the time the contract was made. In contrast, if the amount stated is out of proportion of the likely damages suffered, it will be unlawful and unenforceable.

6.81 In Hong Kong, these principles, as laid down in the classic speech of Lord Dune in *Dunlop Pneumatic Tyre Co Ltd v New Garage & Motor Co Ltd*,[32] are still being applied and have shaped the test to determine whether a clause is one of penalty.

---

32. [1915] AC 79 at 86–88.

6.82 In short, the test is as follows:

(a) It will be held to be a penalty if the sum stipulated for is extravagant and unconscionable in amount in comparison with the greatest loss that could conceivably be proved to have followed from the breach.

(b) It will be held to be a penalty if the breach consists only of not paying a sum of money, and the sum stipulated is a sum greater than the sum which ought to have been paid.

(c) There is a presumption (but no more) that it is penalty when 'a single lump sum is made payable by way of compensation, on the occurrence of one or more of all of several events, some of which may occasion serious and others but trifling damage'.

(d) It is no obstacle to the sum stipulated being a genuine pre-estimate of damages, that the consequences of the breach are such as to make precise pre-estimation almost impossible. On the contrary, that is just the situation when it is probable that pre-estimated damages were the true bargain between the parties.

6.83 Unfortunately, it seems that the above principles have sometimes been applied too literally and, in more recent times, the courts have had to expand the approach to determining what is a penalty and what is a genuine pre-estimate of loss. In the seminal case of *Cavendish Squareholdings v Makdessi*,[33] the UK Supreme Court sets out the proper approach as follows:

> 31. . . . The real question when a contractual provision is challenged as a penalty is whether it is penal, not whether it is a pre-estimate of loss. These are not natural opposites or mutually exclusive categories. A damages clause may be neither or both. The fact that the clause is not a pre-estimate of loss does not therefore, at any rate without more, mean that it is penal. To describe it as a deterrent (or, to use the Latin equivalent, in terrorem) does not add anything. A deterrent provision in a contract is simply one species of provision designed to influence the conduct of the party potentially affected. It is no different in this respect from a contractual inducement. Neither is it inherently penal or contrary to the policy of the law. The question whether it is enforceable should depend on whether the means by which the contracting party's conduct is to be influenced are 'unconscionable' or (which will usually amount to the same thing) 'extravagant' by reference to some norm.

33. [2016] AC 1172. See also *Triple Point Technology Inc v PTT Public Company Ltd* [2021] UKSC 29, where the UK Supreme Court held that an employer would be entitled to liquidated damages that had accrued up to the date of termination of the contract and to general damages after the date of termination.

6.84 As a result, the focus is now on balancing the interest of the innocent party against that determinant placed on the contract-breaker to see whether it is out of proportion.

6.85 However, it should be remembered that, at the time most construction contracts are entered into, it is very difficult, if not impossible, to assess the actual potential loss caused by a breach at the time of the breach.

6.86 Accordingly, in recent times, the Hong Kong courts have adopted the approach in *Cavendish Squareholdings v Makdessi*,[34] including in the recent case of *Brio Electronic Commerce Ltd v Tradelink Electronic Commerce Ltd*.[35] In that case, the contract contained a 'non-solicitation' clause under which the parties agreed not to 'poach' each other's customers. The contract also provided for a sum of HK$5 million for liquidated damages.

6.87 Later, the defendant hired two of the plaintiff's clients. The plaintiff sued the defendant for the HK$5 million damages as prescribed by the contract.

6.88 The defendant argued that the HK$5 million was not payable because it was not a genuine pre-estimate of damages. Naturally enough, it was argued that revenue varied from different clients were different and business from a single major client could be more than the combined business from five other clients. Therefore, it would be difficult, if not impossible, to estimate the loss from losing a client at the time when the contract was signed.

6.89 The Court of Appeal held that, when considering whether such a liquidated damages clause would be valid, one had to consider the matter from the standpoint of the parties at the time when they entered into the contract.

6.90 The court held that, where a breach could have a range of consequences, the clause would be a penalty where the specified amount was extravagant compared with the greatest actual or estimated loss that could be proved to flow from the breach. This approach recognises that the consequences of a breach cannot be foreseen with precision and allows the parties to stipulate for a sum which will provide adequate compensation in the event of breach. Depending on the drafting, the contemplated breach may or may not be expressly read from the contract.

6.91 On the facts of the case, at the time the contract was signed, the plaintiff was very concerned about losing customers as that would seriously affect its survival as a commercial entity. In the circumstances, therefore, an assessment of the likely damage flowing from a breach by reference to two years' commissions was not unreasonable.

34. See also *Ip Ming Kin v Wong Siu Lan* CACV 201/2012 (unreported, 28 May 2013) at [60] and *Law Ting Pong Secondary School v Chen Wai Wah* [2021] HKCA 873.
35. CACV 271/2013 (unreported, 5 May 2016).

6.92 The Court of Appeal also held that the nature of the damages would appear to be the same for potential breaches of the non-solicitation clause. Although the breaches could occur in a number of ways, this was not something that raised a presumption or inference that the sum agreed was a penalty. To hold otherwise would in effect require the parties to estimate in advance the amount of damages payable for every different way in which a breach might occur. This was not what should be expected from the parties from a commercial perspective.

6.93 Thus, the Court of Appeal upheld the liquidated damages clause. Although this judgment confirms that the Hong Kong courts are willing to uphold such clauses, care is needed in the drafting process to avoid clauses being struck down as an unenforceable penalty.

Dispute Resolution Clause

6.94 In most construction contracts in Hong Kong, especially between an employer and the contractor, there is a clause requiring that disputes be referred to an alternative dispute resolution mechanism, setting out the forum and types of disputes to be resolved thereby. Arbitration is a commonly provided for dispute resolution mechanism.

6.95 For example, the General Conditions of Contract for Civil Engineering Works (1999) and the General Conditions of Contract for Building Works (1999) of the Hong Kong Government include arbitration clauses at clause 86.

6.96 While dispute resolution clauses have rarely been given the attention that they deserve and are usually added as an afterthought, the fact is that they are as important as the major contract terms. The purpose of a construction contract is to provide parties with certainty as to their obligations towards each other, and a dispute resolution clause ensures that the parties are given a guideline as to what to do when either party fails to perform or meet such obligations. A failure to consider the dispute resolution clause will lead to a party being at a significant disadvantage during any such dispute.

6.97 Despite the objective of dispute resolution clauses, i.e. to reflect the parties' agreement as to how disputes are to be resolved, in many cases, such clauses (or their drafting) themselves become the subject of a dispute.

6.98 This is highlighted in the recent case *PCCW Global Ltd (formerly Beyond the Network, Ltd) v Interactive Communications Service Ltd (formerly Vectone Ltd)*.[36]

36. [2007] 1 HKLRD 309.

6.99 The dispute stemmed from the drafting of the contract and serves as a good illustration of the effect of a lack of care in drafting dispute resolution clauses.

6.100 The dispute revolved around the following clauses:

> Clause 4: Differences over billing charges were to be resolved amicably between the parties. Failure to reach an amicable resolution within a reasonable period of time (not to exceed 14 days) meant that the parties would submit their differences to the Hong Kong courts for resolution.
>
> Clause 5: The agreement would be subject to the laws of Hong Kong and the parties submitted to the exclusive jurisdiction of the courts of Hong Kong.
>
> Clause 11.2: The agreement would be interpreted in accordance with the laws of the State of New York, and any disputes 'shall be submitted to the courts in the State of New York'.
>
> Clause 11.3: Either party may require any dispute arising under the agreement to be 'settled by binding arbitration in accordance with the commercial arbitration rules of the American Arbitration Association . . . The arbitration shall take place in New York, NY, USA'.

6.101 The primary dispute was over alleged billing discrepancies in invoices issued by the plaintiff to the defendant for the provision of international telephone services. The sum in dispute was US$718,999.26. This led to the plaintiff commencing proceedings against the defendant in the High Court of Hong Kong in December 2004 to recover the disputed sum. The defendant sought to stay the court proceedings on the basis that clause 11.3 was a binding arbitration agreement and therefore, it argued, the court should stay the proceedings in favour of arbitration.

6.102 As many construction professionals may know, Hong Kong is a 'pro-arbitration' jurisdiction and the courts are ready to stay court proceedings and to refer proceedings to arbitration if it is demonstrated that there is, at the very least on the surface, a valid arbitration clause, thus leaving the substantive disputes to the arbitral tribunal.

6.103 At first instance, the court held that clause 11.3, which stipulated for arbitration in New York, was not a binding arbitration agreement and that it was only permissive. Therefore, if there was an additional agreement of the parties that the disputes were to be referred to arbitration, clause 11.3 would override clause 5. However, because the parties did not reach such an agreement to arbitrate, clause 5 remained in effect.

6.104 The court was also of the view that, pursuant to clause 4.3, an attempt by the parties to 'resolve the dispute amicably within a reasonable period of time' included referring the disputes to arbitration under clause 11.3.

6.105 When dealing with contradictions between clause 5 (exclusive jurisdiction of Hong Kong) and clause 11.2 (submission of disputes to the courts of the State of New York), the court found that there was no contradiction because the word 'shall' in clause 11.2 was intended to be permissive and not mandatory.

6.106 In other words, the court found that the word 'shall' in clause 11.2 meant 'may', seemingly contrary to established authorities on interpretation. In coming to this conclusion, the judge placed emphasis on the fact that the alternative would have been to conclude, as argued by plaintiff, that these two clauses gave rise to an insurmountable contradiction and that they should therefore be ignored, thereby leaving the arbitration provision in clause 11.3 as the only clear basis for resolving disputes. However, due to the overriding requirement that the court should 'make sense of the contract as a whole', it placed emphasised the express words of the parties and, accordingly, sought to give them a meaning that worked within the overall contract. The matter was appealed to the Court of Appeal. The Court of Appeal, in essence, agreed with the finding of the court at first instance that this was the only satisfactory answer in the context of the contract as a whole.

6.107 Before the Court of Appeal, the key issue became whether the differences over billing charges that the plaintiff purported to refer to arbitration were in fact covered by clause 11.3, or whether clause 4 provided an exclusive regime to resolve such disputes via the courts of Hong Kong.

6.108 The Court of Appeal answered this question by construing clause 4 and clause 11.3. In the context of the case as a whole and the evidence before the Court of Appeal, it was found that the agreement was initially based on the plaintiff's standard form of contract. The agreement was, however, the result of substantial negotiations leading to a number of drafts being prepared and discussed by the parties.

6.109 It is important to note that the Court of Appeal took into account that it was provided for in the unamended standard form, in relation to differences over billing charges, that 'in the event the parties are unable to resolve the dispute amicably, it shall be resolved by arbitration in accordance with section 11.3'. Those words were replaced during negotiations with the requirement that the differences over billing charges should be dealt with by the courts of Hong Kong. The Court of Appeal found the removal of the arbitration reference to be important in interpreting the clause.

6.110 In the process of deciding whether clause 11.3 covered differences over billing charges, the court analysed the law surrounding the extent of its powers to determine whether there was a valid arbitration agreement. It was argued that the court could determine whether there was a valid arbitration agreement only on a *prima facie* basis and that it should not usurp the functions of the arbitral tribunal to decide the disputes referred to it. The court at first instance had addressed and decided this point by highlighting the significant delay that had already been suffered by the parties since the issue of the writ in December 2004.

6.111 The Court of Appeal took a different route and dealt with the point by looking at the issue of whether there was clear evidence that clause 11.3 gave rise to an arbitration agreement that covered the differences over billing charges. As mentioned above, the Court of Appeal agreed with the conclusion of the first instance court but reasoned that, while clause 11.3 was a permissive but enforceable arbitration agreement, clause 4.3 was a 'self-contained provision on how any dispute or contest over billing should be determined'. It provided for formal notification of disputes and a tight timetable for amicable settlement 'not to exceed 14 days' after which 'then the parties will submit the difference to the Hong Kong Courts'. That being the case, the Court of Appeal concluded that the arbitration agreement in clause 11.3 did not cover disputes over billing charges under clause 4.

6.112 Construction professionals should pay heed to both parties' drafting shortcomings in *PCCW Global Ltd (formerly Beyond the Network, Ltd) v Interactive Communications Service Ltd (formerly Vectone Ltd)*. Parties should always be mindful of the importance of dispute resolution clauses and not overlook them just because disputes seem unlikely. This case also serves as a warning to professionals that, even if something is seemingly insignificant, whether a dispute is to be referred to arbitration can in itself lead to lengthy interlocutory skirmishes.

6.113 Sometimes, perhaps to avoid what happened in *PCCW Global Ltd (formerly Beyond the Network, Ltd) v Interactive Communications Service Ltd (formerly Vectone Ltd)*, contracts in Hong Kong simply include a clause requiring that all disputes are to be referred to arbitration. This again requires careful drafting.

6.114 As an illustration, in the recent case of *Dickson Valora Group (Holdings) Co Ltd and another v Fan Ji Qian*,[37] there was a dispute concerning a joint venture relating to a real estate transaction in Jiangsu, PRC, in relation to a shareholder agreement. A subsequent supplemental agreement and addendum were entered into by some but not all of the signing parties.

6.115 Disputes as to the parties' relationship and allegations of breach of contract culminated in court actions in mainland China unbeknownst to certain parties. Upon finding this out, they mounted an unsuccessful jurisdictional challenge in relation to the mainland court actions. The failure led to a jurisdictional challenge in a different form, in Hong Kong based

37. [2019] HKCFI 48.

on section 21L of the High Court Ordinance (Cap 4), for an injunction to prevent the continuation of the court proceedings in mainland China.

6.116 Lam J (as he then was) granted an injunction, determining that there were four separate issues:

(a) Whether there was an arbitration agreement in the contract being sued upon;

(b) What was the court's approach in the absence of privity of contract in respect of the contract with the arbitration agreement;

(c) Whether there was issue estoppel as result of the jurisdictional challenge to the court actions in mainland China;

(d) Whether there were other reasons in the interest of justice for the injunction not to be granted.

6.117 On the first issue, Lam J determined that there was an arbitration clause as all of the agreements were executed by the same parties and were of complementary nature and purposes. The agreements also did not contain separate provisions on general matters such as choice of law or dispute resolution, which were of particular importance in projects such as these involving people and entities from multiple jurisdictions.

6.118 Lam J also adopted the *Angelic Grace* approach with respect to the court proceedings in mainland China in respect of breach of contract and bringing of 'foreign' proceedings.[38]

6.119 Despite the lack of a governing law clause, Lam J found the contract to be governed by the laws of the Hong Kong but determined that the Contracts (Rights of Third Parties) Ordinance (Cap 623) was not applicable as it came into existence only after the agreement had been executed.

6.120 As to estoppel, Lam J found that, as the decision in the court proceedings in mainland China on jurisdiction was not directly enforceable in Hong Kong, there was no estoppel preventing the parties from challenging jurisdiction again in Hong Kong. Finally, there was no special reason in the interest of justice to refuse the injunction.

6.121 *Dickson Valora Group (Holdings) Co Ltd and another v Fan Ji Qian* serves as a good example of the issues in respect of incorporation of arbitration agreements in the context of a commercial dispute. The latter was a fact the court took into account in its reasoning and its finding that all of the agreements were part and parcel.

38. *The Angelic Grace* [1995] 1 Lloyd's Rep 87. The principles and reasoning in *Angelic Grace* are that the court should feel no diffidence in the grant of an anti-suit injunction to restrain foreign proceedings in breach of an arbitration agreement on the simple and clear ground that the defendant has promised not to bring such proceedings.

6.122 A question arises when there are sequential agreements but a failure to ensure the documents have incorporated all the relevant clauses. As stated in Chapter 5, this is a common mistake in construction contract drafting in Hong Kong.

6.123 A good example is the recent decision in *Yun Kwan Construction Engineering Ltd v Shui Tai Construction Engineering Co Ltd*,[39] where the court was required to deal with the issue of an arbitration clause. The question was whether the contracts between the defendant and its own respective head contractors in two projects had been incorporated into the corresponding contracts between the defendant and the plaintiff.

6.124 In Hong Kong, as it can be seen from Lam J's decision in *Dickson Valora Group (Holdings) Co Ltd and another v Fan Ji Qian*, the law does not necessarily require an arbitration clause to be explicitly referred to to be incorporated. However, whether an arbitration clause has been incorporated will depend on the intentions of the parties, as read from the underlying agreement they have reached.

6.125 In this case, not only were the arbitration clauses between the defendant and its head contractors not referred to in the contract between it and the plaintiff, but the contract documents containing the arbitration clauses were not even provided to the plaintiff.

6.126 This is important as it is common practice in Hong Kong, especially between contractors, to merely refer to or to invite another party to inspect the incorporated contract documents and not to actually provide a copy of those contracts containing the terms intended to be incorporated. This may be due to the voluminous documents involved in upper tier contracts.

Force Majeure/Frustration Clause

6.127 As a result of COVID-19 and other unexpected situations, parties to construction contracts have begun to more seriously examine the content of their contracts to determine whether they have adequate protection in the form of force majeure clauses. In the past, such clauses were not given the attention they deserve.

6.128 Most boilerplate construction contracts contain some form of a force majeure clause. For example, in the standard Hong Kong government contracts, 'special risks' are addressed at clause 84(1), which refers to:

> (a) an outbreak of war (whether war be declared or not) in any part of the world which, whether financially or otherwise materially affects the execution of the Works, or
>
> (b) an invasion of Hong Kong, or

39. [2019] HKCFI 1841.

(c) civil war, rebellion, revolution or military or usurped power in Hong Kong, or

(d) riot, commotion or disorder in Hong Kong otherwise than amongst the employees of the Contractor, any subcontract or Specialist Contractor currently or formerly engaged on the Works or Specialist Works, or

(e) act of foreign terrorists in Hong Kong.

6.129 As it can be seen, this clause only covers the limited situations that are defined to be special risks. This clause also requires the contractor to use best endeavours to complete the execution of the works unless the contract is terminated under the provision.

6.130 If a special event occurs, clause 84(4) provides:

(a) The Contractor shall be under no liability for or in respect of damage to the Works or to property whether of the Employer or of third parties or for or in respect of injury or loss of life which is wholly the consequence of the occurrence of any of the Special Risks and the Employer shall indemnify the Contractor against all such liabilities.

(b) If the Works or any material on the Site shall be destroyed or damaged by reason of any of the Special Risks, the Contractor shall be entitled to payment for the Works and for any materials so destroyed or damaged and the Contractor shall be entitled to recover from the Employer the expense incurred in making good any such destruction or damage to the Works.

(c) Destruction, damage, injury or loss of life caused by the explosion or impact, whenever and wherever occurring, of any mine, bomb, shell, grenade, missile, munition or explosive of war shall be deemed to be a consequence of the special risks.

6.131 As can be seen, such government contracts contemplate some unforeseeable situations, perhaps covering COVID-19. However, some other forms of contracts may not provide force majeure clauses with sufficient coverage of special risks, putting parties at greater risk if unexpected or unforeseeable events do occur.

6.132 Therefore, parties to construction contracts should give serious thought to including properly drafted force majeure clauses in their contracts. In particular, the following non-exhaustive matters should be considered:

- whether extension of time for completion should be granted;
- whether compensation for costs should be allowed;
- what types of special risks should be regarded as events within the operation of such clauses, such as for the reason that they are out of the control of either party;
- how to determine when an event falls within one of those risks.

6.133 At the very least, parties to a construction contract should examine the existing boilerplate clauses, such as clause 84 of the Hong Kong government contracts, to see whether the same or additions thereon should be incorporated into their contracts to fulfil the needs of the parties.

Index

www.ingramcontent.com/pod-product-compliance
Ingram Content Group UK Ltd.
Pitfield, Milton Keynes, MK11 3LW, UK
UKHW021015120926
8556IPUK00040B/1156

9 789888 754113